Social Accounting for Corporations:

Private Enterprise versus the Public Interest

EDITED BY TONY TINKER
Chairman of the Public Interest Section
of the American Accounting Association

with contributions of

CHARLES E. LINDBLOM
Yale University

ABRAHAM J. BRILOFF
Baruch College, City
University of New York

STANLEY SPORKIN
Previously Enforcement
Director, Securities and
Exchange Commission

TONY TINKER
New York University
& Baruch College

Second Printing 1986

For Information write to:
Markus Wiener Publishing, Inc.
2901 Broadway, New York, NY 10025

ISBN 0-910129-17-7

Library of Congress Card Catalog
Card No. 84-051181

Printed in the United States of America

Table of Contents

I.

Introduction

BY TONY TINKER
New York University &
Baruch College, City University of New York

"Public Interest Accounting" is a most unsatisfactory label for describing our particular interests and activities. Are we to conclude from this designation that a "nonpublic interest accounting" exists (Private Interest Accounting)? Does the creation of a separate intellectual realm of "public interest accounting" mean that research and teaching in this area can proceed independently of the remainder of accounting? By hiving off the "public interest" into its own department of knowledge, is there not a danger that we may be relinquishing "accounting proper" to powerful social interests?

For many accountants," public interest accounting" is not an autonomous realm for cultivating "good deeds" and paternalistic liberal ideas; rather, it is a convenient incubation area for developing critical and radical perspectives, intended for populating the subject as a whole. We reject the separation of private and public interests as a spurious dichotomy: all interests are private in so far as they refer to a subset of social members; and all interests are public in that they refer to rights, duties, responsibilities, and obligations that are endowed on social members by virtue of their interrelated roles under a particular social structure (feudalism or capitalism, for instance).

The distinction between "public interest accounting" and "accounting proper" is insidious because it creates a two-tier subject: there is "accounting proper" and, what is, in effect, a residual category--"public interest accounting." Of course, if "accounting proper" attempted to embrace all the social interests that accounting affects, then this two-tier arrangement would be of little consequence. But this is not the case. "Accounting proper" focuses almost exclusively on the interests of a subset of capital providers (certain shareholders, bankers, creditors, etc.), leaving other community members to fend for themselves in the market free-for-all.

The effect, therefore, of perpetuating the distinction between "public interest accounting" and "accounting proper" is to effectively disenfranchise some social interests and give legitimacy and power to others. Orthodox economists have developed an appropriate terminology to describe this disenfranchisement: It is reflected in the concept of "externality." An externality is an economic effect that may be beneficial, but is usually harmful to social members who are "outside" the scope of a particular analysis. Thus while "accounting proper" attends to the interests of a privileged minority of social constituencies, "public interest accounting" is delegated to deal with the leftovers - the residuals or externalities that fall outside the scope of "normal" analysis.

Externalities are instances of that which orthodox accounting selectively excludes from the accounting agenda. Our three distinguished contributors highlight many instances of externalities; they enumerate a variety of ways in which accountants and auditors have become willing servants of partisan interests by supporting the exploitation of certain social constituencies on behalf of others. In the final paper, I review the various forms of domination and exploitation that accountants aid-and-abet, and attempt to develop a comprehensive framework (based on the theory of alienation) that enables us to see both the relevance of our contributors' proposals and the forms of alienation, perpetuated by accounting practice, that presently pass unrecognized by the public interest and social accounting literature.

The papers in this volume are not offered in the spirit of contributions to an intellectual backwater called "public interest accounting"; they are direct challenges to mainstream accounting theory and practice. Professors Briloff, Lindblom, as well as Mr. Sporkin are renown authorities in very different fields, yet there are striking similarities between their perspectives. They share a common concern about the way accounting academia and practice have been compromised; about the self-serving ways of defining problems and conceptualizing issues; about the lack of independence of a profession of social adjudicators and arbiters whose most precious asset is its integrity and evenhandedness.

I will not attempt to paraphrase the papers offered by our three contributors, but only wish to underscore the importance of what is being said. What our authors highlight are contradictions and antagonisms that are ever-present. The forms of exploitation and domination under discussion here (abuse of investors, customers, neighborhoods, labor, third world countries, etc.) are neither ephemeral nor costless to our social system. These appropriative practices may be sublimated for a while, but their deleterious affects will reemerge in the guise of new social neuroses, and will eventually require the kind of diagnosis that is offered here.

The following chapters are drawn from the proceedings of a symposium organized by the Public Interest Section of the American Accounting Association in 1982 in San Diego. Several people made outstanding contributions to this venture: the marketing function was handled by Diane Darby, Bruce Koch, Barbara Merino, Marilyn Neimark, and Gary Neimark (we mailed over two thousand flyers). Scott Cowan - the then chairman of the Public Interest Section - demonstrated superb management skills by delegating everything and then keeping well out of sight. Tom Burns and Paul Gerhardt provided excellent administrative support right up to the date of the symposium. Millie Taylor not only handled a big part of the word processing, but navigated the difficult terrain of "downtown NYU" with a level of diplomacy that earns my vote for her as GBA dean. I am extremely grateful to Donna Montanino for typing the bulk of the book in the face of extreme adversity; she not only displayed maturity and commonsense, but did so with a delightful disposition that has made this project a pleasure to work on. In the same vein, I am most grateful to Janice, Bebbi, and Karan for their support. Markus Wiener not only published this book, he also offered extensive suggestions about content and style. Markus is not a commercial publisher, he is - first and foremost - an academic publisher who cares a great deal about words and ideas; I am most grateful for his contributions to this book. If someone is to be credited with the success of the whole operation, it is my colleague Marilyn Neimark: I was very fortunate indeed to find intellectual, diplomatic, and managerial skills all compounded into such a small person. Her counsel throughout this project proved to be of the highest caliber. I am especially indebted to our three main speakers - Abraham Briloff, Charles Lindblom and Stanley Sporkin - for their contributions to this endeavor; as editor, I accept ultimate responsibility for all errors contained in the work. Finally, thanks are due to all the large accounting firms who, despite their reputation as public institutions, refused to give any support for this public interest venture. (There was one firm that did support us as long as it was granted anonymity). Their behavior helps to underscore the importance of small projects such as this: all is not well when a major public profession can afford lavish cocktail parties, overrunning with pink gin, but resist a modest inquiry into its relation to the public interest.

Tony Tinker
Baruch College and New York University,
April 1984

II.

The Accountability of Private Enterprise: Private-No: Enterprise-Yes

BY CHARLES E. LINDBLOM
Yale University

On corporate responsibility--there was a time when a Colonel Vanderbilt could say, "The public be damned," and when Mr. Baer, the mining executive, could declare that God in his infinite wisdom had given stewardship of the nation's resources to men of property. Both displayed an insensitivity to public accountability or responsibility, as though enterprises were wholly private organizations and consequently could be run simply as their managements saw fit.

Presumably Colonel Vanderbilt did not wholly damn the public. He apparently only meant to censure interference with some of his financial operations. He must have known, as every businessman knows, that the whole point of a business enterprise is in a sense to discharge a public responsibility. That is, a business exists to try to produce a product or a service. If it cannot produce a product or a service, it cannot survive. That fundamental fact of responsibility even Colonel Vanderbilt recognized.

In any case, businessmen speak today in more conciliatory terms a few irritated exceptions aside from time to time. Today we have two main arguments about the responsibility of business enterprise.

One is that we, the public, can achieve sufficient accountability from and control over the corporation by the device that we sometimes call "voting with dollars." That is to say, we can hold corporations responsible because we, as consumers, have the success or failure of each enterprise in our hands. It either produces what we want or it goes out of business.

The second argument is brought up as a counter to the criticism that corporations are too exclusively responsible stockholders and not sufficiently responsible to other groups. It is that corporate executives are now educated and sophisticated to enlarge the scope of their responsibility to include the work force, customers, suppliers, creditors, and all participants in the production process. That being so, we can now count on a broader responsibility than ever before.

I shall look at each of these two arguments in turn. First, however, I want to suggest that we all agree that indeed there has to be some kind of substantial systematic control over the corporation. Notice that I do not say what kind. I do not necessarily governmental control--only control. I mean control in the broad sense in which social scientists use the term. It could be a control achieved for some groups by professional standards, or it could be marketplace control, or it could be governmental control. Do we not all agree that, for any organization as substantial as a corporation, with a function of importance to the whole society, with decisions being made at the executive level of great importance to many different groups, an axiomatic proposition is that there has to be some method of sustained control over that organization.

Now we will look at the two arguments. Will we get the control that is required through voting with dollars, or through the soulful corporation that acknowledges a broader responsibility than merely to its stockholders? The first argument—on voting with dollars—has an enormous hole in it. Curiously, the hole in the argument is not systematically recorded in the literature of economics or anywhere else (though you know that the hole exists as well as I do). To identify it is not going to tell you anything new, but I will ask you to acknowledge that you know something that you did not know you knew.

Voting with dollars is a scheme of consumer control or customer control over the supplier. Ask yourself, "What does it cover?" It covers, of course, the product. That is, you and I as consumers, as well as industrial buyers, have control over the product. If we do not get, roughly at least, the product we want, we do not have to buy. Granted, there are possibilities of buyer control, for example, monopolistic exploitation of the buyer, but basically, it is a device that works roughly and can be improved for control over the product.

Buyers can require that the seller give us what we want in quantity, general design, and product quality, provided we have a way (as we often do) of discriminating between the low and the high quality products. When we cannot discriminate, and for some complex goods we cannot, we lose a measure of control. But, in principle, we have a control mechanism over quantity and quality of product.

But what about control over plant location? What is there in the scheme of voting with dollars that gives us control over plant location? We do not even know where the plant is located when we buy most products. And what about production technology? Suppose that the technology causes toxic waste disposal or leads to any other of several possible adverse environmental effects? Although we can go to political channels or occasionally organize a boycott, there is not anything in ordinary voting with dollars, nothing in ordinary buyer control, that permits us to distinguish between products that have adverse environmental technologies and those that do not. We may not even know about environmental effects of a given technology. Yet even if we knew, there is no effective way to use buyer control. Among other difficulties, many who might suffer the environmental effects are not among potential customers.

Why have we traditionally believed that buyer control is effective when, in fact, it is inoperative for many aspects of a business? I think the answer is that for a long time we assumed that how a product was produced, where it was produced, how the work force was organized, how the executives were recruited and paid, and all the other secondary factors in production, were of no concern to the buyer as long as these decisions were made economically. That is to say, we assumed, for the conventional concept of market control, that buyers were interested in choosing products at low cost but were otherwise unconcerned about the production process. Competition among sellers we counted on not only to put pressure on the seller to give us what we wanted, but to do it cheaply. Buyer control was, in addition to control over product quantity and quality, an effective program of regulating the one dimension that we cared about concerning technology, plant location, and all these secondary aspects of production--that it be cheap.

But now we live in a world in which these secondary issues are no longer secondary. We do not want products to be too cheaply produced, if cheap means that corporations are going to use technologies, or choose plant locations, or make other decisions that result in adverse effects for buyers. Let me call the decisions that once were secondary, "delegated" choices. I choose the word "delegated" because they have been delegated to the corporation not subject to control through voting with dollars. Dollars do not vote on those delegated issues. That is the big hole in our system of social control over the corporation. It is an extraordinary feature of the corporate economy: A system in which corporate executives make decisions of urgent and first-rate importance to our health, safety, prosperity, welfare and happiness, over which the market system offers no method of social control other than pressure toward cost reduction.

Let us look at the second of the two arguments: that corporations are sufficiently responsible. It is that corporation executives are now sufficiently sophisticated and informed to enlarge the scope of their responsibility from stockholder alone to all other persons whose welfare is affected by corporate decisions.

Stop and think how to interpret that argument. It is in effect a defense or proposal for benevolent despotism. It ought to call up in your minds all the traditional arguments against the tired old notion that elites can be trusted to be wise and benevolent. In the political arena, it is an argument that we have historically rejected, resoundingly and conclusively, in the tradition of the rise of western democracy. We no longer bother to entertain the possibility that presidents and congressmen could be counted on to be sufficiently benevolent to look after us in the absence of the vote and other devices through which we can put them out of office and in other ways influence what they do.

That being so, it seems ludicrous to debate seriously the notion that corporate leadership can be counted on to be benevolent in the absence of systematic and powerful social controls over them.

Any objections to that? Do you want to say that the powers that are in the hands of businessmen are minor relative to the powers that are in the hands of public officials? So minor that we can count on benevolence? Ask yourself: Is it really the business powers that are minor? Let me state some of the important decisions: The organization of the work force, its allocation, the various lines of production to be pursued, the organization of particular industries, the allocation of new investment, the organization of the nation's transportation and communication, and the level of employment. Who makes these decisions? The answer is that, although these decisions are all peripherally regulated by government, the immediate and proximate policymakers on all those major decisions are businessmen, corporate executives for the most part.

If you look at the big coordinating, moving, organizing functions in our society, you see that they are divided between two groups of leaders--government affiliates and businessmen. The latter are no less consequential than the former. I traveled from Los Angeles to San Diego today in a low-flying plane. I could see the configuration of the landscape. Man's architecture and engineering is everywhere visible. Which man? Primarily businessmen. It was their work, not that of government officials, that had restructured the surface of the earth. By any test that you use, businessmen are, in their consequences for our welfare and happiness, equal to that of government officials. Not long ago, we would have laughed out of court the notion that government officials can be counted on to be benevolent without our economic controls over them. We need to give the same treatment to the notion that corporation management will voluntarily assume a benevolent, broad responsibility. Moreover, a would-be benevolent corporate executive is under specific pressure to forget benevolence. He is constantly under pressure to cut costs.

With respect to our two arguments then, the first on voting with dollars and the second on voluntary responsibility, we do not have the basics of corporate responsibility. It is, therefore, inevitable and desirable that we come to see that we shall have to greatly increase the scope of government regulation of business enterprise. There seems to be no alternative.

We shall consequently have to abandon the traditional view that corporations are private organizations. We shall have to acknowledge the public character of enterprises, especially of big businesses (and by big I mean not the biggest, but anything but the very smallest kinds of business enterprises). We shall have to acknowledge that they have become social instruments in the same way that government agencies are social instruments.

I can anticipate obvious objections to such a conclusion. One is that the record of public regulation is on many counts poor and the costs of it too high. We have been hearing that message from many quarters in the last two or three years.

None of these people who are doing cost-benefit analysis on the cost of public regulation have ever turned their analytical tools on the presidency, or the army, or the congress, all of which, it might be argued, are ineffective on cost-benefit grounds. We know, however, that we must have these institutions. Similarly, even at high cost there is no escape from deploying instruments of social control over the corporation.

We might also ask why the costs of governmental regulation of business are so high and the task so difficult to do well. Its difficulties, its inordinate conflict over it, its frequent ineffectiveness, and its cost are for some large part, a constant struggle of businessmen to render regulation ineffective, to fight it off, and to discredit it.

We have always put more executive, legal, accounting, and political talent into frustrating public regulation in the United States than in making it work.

Constitutional protections of due process and of private property give the adversaries of public regulation a powerful tool with which to obstruct it, raise its costs, and discredit it, as in the recent discrediting of the Federal Trade Commission.

We cannot, therefore, accept the record of constitutionally based obstruction to public regulation and the consequent inefficacy and high cost of regulation as eternal facts of life, planted in the soul of man. The difficulties are planted in the American legal and constitutional tradition, from which many of them can be removed.

I come finally to a point of particular relevance for the accounting profession. If there is to be good regulation, there has to be disclosure. We have to get the facts; we have to know what goes on in the business enterprise. By the "we" I mean the public and governmental regulators.

The tradition of proprietor privacy and of trade secrets has militated against disclosure of the information that we need for regulation. That would seem to suggest that we must breed a profession, or reform a profession, or encourage an existing profession - a profession of financial investigators - for looking within the corporation. This leads to an invitation to the accounting profession to move its prestigious core away from identification with the private sector's sectorial interests, which include interests in obstructing regulation, and identifying its prestigious core with a growing role in social investigation for the benefit of responsible authority and accountable corporations.

Discussion

OF

THE ACCOUNTABILITY OF PRIVATE ENTERPRISE

PRIVATE - NO, ENTERPRISE - YES

PARTICIPANTS IN THE DISCUSSION

OF

CHARLES LINDBLOM'S

PAPER

Wayne G. Bremser, Villanova University

Scott S. Cowan, Case Western Reserve University

Peter S. Goodrich, University of Leeds (UK)

Jeffrey L. Harkins, University of Idaho

Maurice Moonitz, University of California at Berkeley

Francis B. Tims, California State University - Hayward

QUESTIONER 1: I come from England, a country which according to myth is said to be more regulated than the USA. I just returned from a trip to Scandinavia. Norway, Sweden, Denmark, and Finland are also mythologically more regulated than the United States. It seems to me that the problem may not be more regulation but better regulation. It seems to me also that Professor Lindblom is primarily addressing the United States model. I would like to know his experiences from a comparative political situation, and also the fact that in some countries, notably Scandinavia, we have a system of more regulation, more government control. For example, in Finland you must make sure that when you put a junkyard up it is completely surrounded by a fence and wall; it must be obstructed from view by pine trees. I mention the myth about more regulations in other countries because I am doing some studies on international accounting using Price-Waterhouse data. The United States far and away has more accounting requirements by legislation than any other country. They are about 20 percent higher than in any other country--64 nations studied. So I think it is a bit of a myth in the U.S. that business is more, if you want, free or less regulated than in other countries. I think it is really a question of slight differences in quantity.

What I ask is why do some countries, notably Scandinavian countries, seem to have better quality of regulation in terms of the general appearance and economic development of their societies, whereas another country, like England, seems to be lagging somewhat.

CHARLES LINDBLOM: You have actually asked several questions. Is the need for more control, or better control? I do not know just how to draw the distinction, but effective control is not simply a matter of piling on more regulations. There have to be some design and skill in it. An example: In my town of North Haven, Connecticut, we have a chemical plant discharging pollutants into a river and also discharging an odorous, eye-irritating chemical into the air. Neighbors have, for several years now, organized in order to obtain disclosure of what these discharges consist of. They have been unsuccessful. The company claims proprietary rights. Now it is quite possible that the State Environmental Protection Agency actually has the authority to require full disclosure, but they are afraid that, if they press the company too hard, it will move the plant out of the state of Connecticut. That is the story over and over again in the United States and indeed in European countries too: The efficacy of control in actual fact is constantly reduced by the standing fear of governments that businesses will stop production or move elsewhere. Do we need in these cases more control or better control? It is a little hard to separate the idea of more and better. I very much agree with the suggestion that runs through your whole statement that there are vast differences in the skill with which regulation is undertaken and that some countries do better. As to those differences, it is a long story as to why some of the Scandinavian countries, for example, can carry off some kinds of regulation better than we can. For one thing, there is less of a constitutional protection in many European countries for the rights of the corporation then there is in the United States. There are also differences arising out of a political culture. I was in Sweden about a month ago, and I was deeply impressed with one subtle, nondocumentable difference. Swedes look upon Americans, many Swedes told me, as wild men in their disrespect for the collective interest. When you stand American attitudes toward public authority, private interest, and cooperative group interests against Scandinavian attitudes, you see two different cultures. Old historical roots apparently account for these differences.

QUESTIONER 2: You drive across the country, you see some of the steel mills closed because they do not have money to modernize. Stockholders obviously do not want to reinvest so we are gradually letting this basic industry almost die, and we are buying from Japan and wherever. How would you see this situation being dealt with? By government subsidies to the steel industry?

CHARLES LINDBLOM: I think it is quite possible that we ought to let the steel industry die. I cannot claim to know enough about our particular comparative advantage in steel but, as you know, it is now being suggested that that kind of industrial process is one in which we have particular strengths relative to other countries and that we ought to move from steel into high technology lines of production or even, and it seems surprising, out of steel into agriculture. But if on national defense grounds, or some other ground like that, we decided we want a steel industry, then, it seems to me that we may have to subsidize it. There is a good case, incidentally, for extending scrutiny and disclosure if we are going to put public funds heavily into maintenance of any industry. We are going to have to cope with great pressures put on governments to bail out and support dying industries. We shall have to be hard-hearted about letting industries die that have outlived their usefulness.

QUESTIONER 3: I would like to turn to your closing remarks about the need for developing a profession to do the kind of disclosure that you are sketching for us, or to redo the existing profession and if you have any ideas of how this can be done with the existing profession and see if you have any ideas of how this can be done with the existing groups, particularly the American Institute of CPA's, in which as far back as I can remember, one of the ways in which the leadership of the Institute has been able to get some so-called self-regulation in place, has been to raise the specter of government regulations. In other words, the final blow, the final argument to convince the members to fall in line, is that if we do not do it, Washington will. And that would be terrible. How can we work to change this very deep cultural approach of the organization which represents the accounting profession; is there anything out of general organizational behavior of social groups that can help us to bring about change in an attitude that is so deep-seated?

CHARLES LINDBLOM: That is a tough question to ask anybody who does not know the accounting profession very well. There does not seem to be much chance of reforming your or any profession by any one or a few formulae. A profession is more likely to be reformed by slow-moving incremental alterations in its opportunities or in its own introspective sense of its responsibilities. You seize on opportunities as they historically open up because of controversies over what the profession is doing, or new difficulties of clients that call for new practices. Among the incremental reforms well worth considering is the organization of this new section of your association to which we owe today's meeting.

QUESTIONER 3: Is there anything in the history of other professions? For example, medicine comes to mind, which, at the national level, has probably been much more powerful than the accountants in resisting the encroachment of any kind of explicit, social regulation.

CHARLES LINDBLOM: Now are you asking how the accounting professions can escape governmental regulations?

QUESTIONER 3: I accepted your goals for purposes of discussion right now, I accept your goals that we ought to—we must—have a professional group which is capable of doing the technical job of getting the disclosure that you would like to see: Improved increased disclosure, more accurate disclosure.

CHARLES LINDBLOM: Much of the development of the profession of medicine, it seems to me, has been to make medicine irresponsible rather than responsible. It has been responsible along one dimension in the United States: high technical quality of service. But on its response to other public needs and on the distribution of its resources and its energy,it has a very poor record of responsibilities. At the same time, it has an excellent record in fending off any attempt to alter the profession. Medical services are a matter of great and urgent concern to everyone. It is, therefore, possible for the profession to mobilize voters with public campaigns, and it is also possible for the medical profession to play on all kinds of fears of irresponsibility. Accountants lack the intimacy of connection with the public. Your public is largely the business community and that means you are constantly being held to and judged by their standards.

QUESTIONER 3: That is true. It also could be a strength if we wanted to work quietly within the accounting profession without the glare of public scrutiny.

CHARLES LINDBLOM: Yes, but given the sort of privacy and intimacy of the connection between business management and accountants, would it not be a kind of act of treason to begin to work privately and secretly to make business more accountable?

QUESTIONER 4: My question is really a follow-up. I am very sympathetic with your arguments that there is a greater incentive to thwart existing accounting and legal regulations. I am sympathetic with that because I believe there is an economic incentive for business to attempt to do that, to lower costs, if you will. But I see the problem that you raise is really a dilemma for accountants of philanthropy versus finance. It is nice, from a public interest point of view, to be sympathetic to the notion that we ought to have a different set of rules, we ought to provide for full disclosure. But the question I really pose to you then is who pays for the alternative, who pays for that? Because right now there is a strong economic incentive to hire the very best legal and finance minds to thwart the regulation. And a quick solution might be to find the funding source to hire those same minds in an advocate position that you propose.

CHARLES LINDBLOM: It seems to me that social scientists, accountants, lawyers, and other supposedly informed people, have simply not attended seriously to that question. How does one finance a rectification of the gross imbalance in the legal and accounting professions? The problem derives from the relative poverty of the regulators and wealth of the regulatees. I mean that literally. We have hardly begun to think about such a possibility as constraining business expenditure for the legal and accounting services. We have not thought about a variety of possibilities that seem to run against constitutional protections of free speech and other constitutional protections of individual liberty. But when you begin to think of the corporation as a kind of public agency, though not a governmental agency, then it makes sense to ration out funds in the adversary relationship to bring about something closer to a balance in the adversaries' resources. That kind of a proposal is perhaps shocking because it challenges long-established prerogatives that we have not been interested in challenging. Yet we all have a stake in how a corporation uses its resources. Where does it get its financial resources? From you and me--from all of us. It is an organization which draws on the incomes of all of us as certainly as taxes draw on our incomes. And just as we do insist through public accountability of government officials on control over the expenditure of tax funds for certain purposes, it is quite conceivable we might find a way to impose regulations on business enterprise with respect to the amount of funds they can put into adversarial work. Similarly, we might consider such possibilities as forbidding corporate enterprise to use its funds for anything but what might narrowly be called production. That is to say, consider restricting or forbidding the expenditure of corporate funds for obstructing legislation, restricting or prohibiting the corporation from giving any of its funds away to universities, to research groups, teams, museums, civic centers, orchestras, or anything of the sort. Corporate philanthropic spending of your and my money is in some senses an odd practice.

We might want to make of the corporation a specialist in doing what it does well, rather than leaving it so free to indulge its taste for a whole variety of activities.

QUESTIONER 5: As a rationale or a technique, what do you think of federal chartering of corporations rather than state chartering as an occasional disciplinary action such as a revocation of a public charter?

CHARLES LINDBLOM: I cannot say that it is an issue that has greatly engaged me, but it seems to me that it is a quite reasonable proposal. It is possible there might be a case on administrative grounds for big organizations. For large organizations that have national repercussions on markets, there is not a great case, it seems to me, for perpetuating state authority.

Double Entry: Double Think: Double Speak

BY ABRAHAM J. BRILOFF
Baruch College, City University of New York

Introduction

"Double Entry: Double Think: Double Speak." Clearly, that title was inspired by the Orwellian fantasy: Nineteen Eighty-Four. All too frequently, sadly so, my study of auditors' footnotes and even promulgations from the Financial Accounting Standards Board remind me of the Orwellian precepts: Emblazoned on its Ministry of Truth:

Ignorance is Strength

War is Peace

Slavery is Freedom.

The theme "Accountants in the Public Interest" can have many facets, for example:

Accountancy in the Public Sector

Accounting for Human Resources

Social Audits.

All of these are aspects of accounting and of our profession's responsibility; without detracting one iota from their importance I have determined, nonetheless, to concentrate on what I believe to be the single most important, transcendent responsibility of our profession, i.e., the independent, external audit of publicly-owned corporations.

It is because these giant multinational entities represent concentrations of enormous pools of resources, human, material, and ecological, that they demand our very special attention. These entities are possessed of such extraordinary power that to help avoid the abuse of that power, the true, objective history of the manner of its exercise needs to be written. In short, the independent, external audit is presumed to help obviate Lord Acton's foreboding that, "Power corrupts, and absolute power corrupts absolutely."

"Fighting the figures and finding the facts"

To help assure the integrity of corporate management and of the communications to the world of investors, creditors and others who have a vital stake in the conduct of these corporate enterprises, we have, over the past half century at least, institutionalized the independent, external audit function. The spirit of the independent auditor's role was best captured by the late Colonel Robert H. Montgomery who asserted, "It is (the accountant's) duty, after fighting the figures and finding the facts, to assemble the figures and tell the truth about them, with clarity, conciseness and intelligence . . . ."

To help assure the effectiveness of that process, we have, over the decades, developed a series of "concentric rings" of regulatory and self-regulatory agencies. Thus, moving outwards from the auditor we have his various apparatus, the POB, the FASB, etc. We then have the several Federal and State regulatory bodies, especially in this context, the SEC. The next outer ring in our constellation is the judiciary, administering the various securities laws and the common law. Finally, we have the Congress of the United States which, in the first instance, acts as the lawgiver and then, as an incident to its investigative activities, can and may fulfill an oversight role over the accounting profession and its audit function.

Most assuredly, if this complex system were, in fact, operating anywhere near optimally, there would be little basis for the title theme of this presentation.

Why do I take the occasion of this visit to the AAA convention in San Diego for lamentation? Essentially because, in my view, this elaborate system of concentric rings, of presumptive checks and balances, is not functioning to assure the fulfillment of the objectives of the financial reporting process--and what gives me even greater concern is that I sense that the system is heading for further deterioration and possibly even disintegration.

That my concerns are not merely those of a present-day Jeremiah, I point to a feature article in the Wall Street Journal of July 9, 1982, entitled "Accounting Scams Are on the Rise, Putting More Pressure on Auditors." That article alluded to audit failures at Penn Square, JWT (J. Walter Thompson), Datapoint Corp., Flight Transportation Corporation. I turn then to the fleshing out of my anxious concerns.

First, regarding the Auditing Standards Board:

I will first consider the AICPA's Auditing Standards Board. A couple of years ago, the Board exposed for consideration by the Institute's membership a revised form of standard audit report which, if adopted, would have read as follows:

INDEPENDENT AUDITOR'S REPORT

The accompanying balance sheet of X Company as of (at) December 31, 19XX, and the related statements of income, retained earnings and changes in financial position for the year then ended are management's representations. An audit is intended to provide reasonable, but not absolute, assurance as to whether financial statements taken as a whole are free of material misstatements. We have audited the financial statements referred to above in accordance with generally accepted auditing standards. Application of those standards requires judgment in determining the nature, timing and extent of tests and other procedures, and in evaluating the results of those procedures.

Opinion Paragraph

In our opinion, the financial statements referred to above present the financial position of X Company as of (at) December 31, 19XX, and the results of its operations and the changes in its financial position for the year then ended are in conformity with generally accepted accounting principles.

As we know, the Institute's Auditing Standards Board which had proposed the foregoing revised Auditor's report determined, after having been inundated with letters of sharp criticism, to abort this misbegotten venture. For me, this ASB expedition, aided and abetted by the AICPA executive who played an important role in the writing of the Cohen Commission report, should not now be deemed a "trial balloon" which was shot down. Instead, that venture tells me that in the highest places in our profession's hierarchy there sit persons who do not have the vision required to lead us to the fulfillment of our awesome responsibilities to the citizenry of our economic and political society.

It is essential that you recognize that the ASB was not, by this proposal, presuming to change the prevailing standards governing the audit. If the truth be told, there was a salutary aspect to the proposal. Thus, at the least, the public would have been informed of the only most limited responsibility which the independent auditor assumes as an incident to his rendering a "clean opinion."

Note that the proposal would have made abundantly clear that the statements are management's and not the auditor's. Further, there would have been a fair inference drawn from the deletion of the "fairness" phrase that the auditor is not assuring the public that the statements are, in fact, fair.

A Complementary Development

This self-exculpatory proclivity is complemented by the

growing tendency on the part of management explicitly to absolve the independent auditor of much of the responsibility presumed to be vested in him by society. Thus, we now may find a so-called Report from Management which states essentially that which the ASB proposal sought to set forth, and then proceeds further to set forth the expanded turf of management, correspondingly limiting that of the auditor.

Included herein as Appendix A is the report from management included in General Electric's 1981 annual report.

Consistent with the abdication to the corporation of significant portions of the responsibilities presumed to have been vested in the auditor we find the evolving audit committee of boards of directors.

This development could have a most significant effect on the entire process of corporate governance. The challenges and my misgivings relating to this development are beyond the scope of this presentation; they are borne out, however, in Section 3.5 of the American Law Institute's recently promulgated Restatement of Principles of Corporate Governance and Structure.

Corrupting the FCPA

Also with regard to my misgivings concerning the prevailing independent audit environment I despair at observing the ways in which our colleagues have contributed to the corruption of the Foreign Corrupt Practices Act of 1977

("FCPA"). That enactment was designed to put an end to what President Carter described as ethically repugnant conduct by American enterprise. Along with prohibiting companies from engaging in certain corrupt practices with respect to foreign officials, the Act amended Section 13(b) of the Securities Exchange Act of 1934 to require reporting companies to make and keep accurate books and records, and to establish and maintain a system of internal accounting controls. Surely, this enactment should have evoked a hosanna from our profession's Establishment. Instead, we found the Institute in the vanguard of various endeavors to dilute the FCPA's objectives.

I urge that you study the Smith-Jacobson decision in the Tax Court of the United States (March 5, 1982), and the New York Times February 18, 1982 (relating to Merrill Lynch and Citicorp, respectively) and then to join with me in impeaching our profession's leadership for not speaking out forthrightly and aggressively against these overt manifestations of what I believe to be the corruption of the internal control systems in those bastions of high finance, and then to impeach our Institute's hierarchy for their having aided and abetted the corruption of the Foreign Corrupt Practices Act of 1977.

Several months ago, we were let in on another manifestation of gross misfeasance, nonfeasance, malfeasance and/or reckless irresponsibility--this time it had to do with the giant Chase Manhattan Bank making available to a fledgling, minimally capitalized, Drysdale Government Securities Corporation some $4 billion of U.S. Treasury securities. We were told that the bank would be sustaining an after-tax loss presently estimated at $135 million—a loss that would be spread among Chase's shareholders and employees. We were also informed that the Financial Establishment had now learned a lesson, i.e., "to know the borrower."

What seems to have been overlooked is that the public at large has been victimized by Chase's irresponsibility. Remember, we are absorbing the other half of the hole in the doughnut—the $135 million by which Chase would be reducing its already infinitesimal tax contribution to the Federal Treasury.

For me this whole fiasco is yet another manifestation of a breakdown of internal control—a breakdown for which Chase's management and its independent auditors should be made to respond.

Nor will I accept the glib response that $135 million (or twice that number) is, for Chase, a mere bagatelle. A publicly-owned entity by its very nature implies a fiduciary responsibility—a banking institution all the more so.

For the past half dozen years, I have written extensively and traveled the nation from north to south and east to west lamenting what I believed to be a most egregious misapplication of accounting precepts discerned by me. In testimony before the Congress and in various addresses, I have appealed to the audiences to help me rationalize the accounting by the Lockheed Aircraft Corporation (with Arthur Young's imprimatur) for its ill-fated L-1011, TriStar-Program.

To the present, I have received no response to AY's testimony before the Metcalf Committee in 1977. I have maintained that AY's testimony presented the Senate with cropped data and challenged the firm to an open discourse regarding the issues--thus far without response.

I am now here in San Diego, in Lockheed's backyard, and I sincerely hope that the insights, the response which would set my soul at rest, might here be forthcoming. Thus, there must be some accounting precepts peculiar to this area which are unknown to those who have spent their lifetimes in the more bucolic New York regions.

To this end, I have included as Appendix B the Lockheed Airbus(t) Saga. Please help.

The FASB Bogged Down

We are led, then, to the Financial Accounting Standards Board—the Stamford Think Tank which is presumed to resolve the Herculean theoretical challenges confronting the profession.

Over the past nineteen months, the FASB has promulgated an equal number of statements which it has dubbed, pretentiously, I submit, statements of standards. What subjects were covered by these awesome pronouncements numbered 45 through 63? I have catalogued them into three sections, to wit: (1) those that relate to a particular industry and are, accordingly, nought but industry guides; (2) elaborations, amendments, revisions, etc., regarding earlier statements; and (3) statements regarding the application (or precluding a misapplication) of a previous precept, or mandating further disclosure.

Essential Industry Guides:

SFAS No.	Industry
45	Franchisors
50	Record and Music
51	Cable Television
53	Motion Picture Film Distributors
56	Contractors and Hospital-Related Operations
60	Insurance Entities
61	Title Plant
63	Broadcasters

Revision, Application or Interpretation of Previously Promulgated SFAS:

SFAS No.	Prior SFAS No.	Topic
46	33	Motion Picture Films
52	8	Foreign Currency Translation
54	33	Investment Companies
55	(APB) 15	Common Stock Equivalents
58	34	Re Equity Accounting
59	35	Deferral of Implementation re Governmental Units
62	34	Interest Cost Where Tax-Exempt Borrowings Are Involved

Promulgation of a Rule for Application of GAAP and/or Disclosure of the Practice:

SFAS No.	Topic
47	Disclosure of Long-Term Obligations
48	Revenue Recognition where Right of Return Exists
49	Product Finance Arrangements
57	Related Party Disclosures

By way of recapitulation: We have no fewer than eight presumptive standards devoted to the rules for particular industries; an equal number are devoted to revising, interpreting, amplifying or applying a previously-promulgated presumptive standard. Leaving but four (of the nineteen promulgated between January 1, 1981 and mid-1982) for what is euphemistically referred to as standard setting. These four, note once again, and to what are these four milestones devoted?

To repeat:

47 - Disclosure of Long-Term Obligations
48 - Regarding Receivable Where Rights of Return Exists
49 - Product-Financing Arrangements
57 - Related-Party Transactions

Standards? Humbug!

The Standard for Standards

In determining whether there is anything in them deserving of the encomium of a "standard," I ask that you pause a moment to reflect on the meaning of that critical term. Let us examine what Paton and Littleton said in that regard:

> Standards should deal more with fundamental conceptions, general approaches to the presentation of accounting facts than with questions of precise captions, degrees of subdivision, and detailed methods of estimating . . . .
>
> . . . . It should be possible to state accounting standards in such a way that they will be useful guides to procedures over a wide area of application. Whereas rules would be made to afford a basis for conformity, standards are conceived as gauges by which to measure departures, when and if departure is necessary and clearly justifiable. Standards, therefore, should not prescribe procedures or rigidly confine practices; rather standards should serve as guideposts to the best in accounting report . . . .

True, the much tortured Foreign Currency Translation Statement No. 52 will be tossed up as a "standard." Is it really? Is it nought but an arbitrary, compromised, and potentially capricious rule?

More recently, writing in the March, 1982, issue of

Accounting Education News, Professor William A. Paton sharply criticized the FASB for its failure to promulgate standards qua standards. According to the accounting professor (who began teaching the subject seventy years ago):

> . . . The "Accounting Principles Board" shortly edged in the direction of laying down the law, telling what we could or could not do. And now we have the "Financial Accounting Standards Board," a very formal body, well supplied with funds, issuing dated orders, with an air of supreme authority. The justification for the FASB (and similar bodies representing groups of professionals somewhat concerned with accounting) commonly advanced is that dictation by the Board, cooperating with government agencies where possible, is much more acceptable than outright regulation by government. This position may have some merit, but I cannot applaud. It seems to me that the FASB is doing a lot of floundering, fussing with details that should be left alone and delaying unduly reaching final conclusions on basic isues. Perhaps I am too critical.
>
> The surge of regulation, in which the FASB has joined with its prescribed "standards," is having an adverse effect on instruction in accounting. Textbooks nowadays are often heavily loaded with outlines of the prevailing rules affecting accounting practice, and learning the rules tends to be the student's major objective. This is a poor substitute for an intensive study of a system of concepts and procedures designed to provide business executives, and the investors to whom they are responsible, with the financial information essential to sound operation.

In a corresponding mood, when Professor William T. Baxter delivered his Emanuel Saxe Distinguished Lecture at Baruch College in February, 1979, he lamented the anti-intellectualism which presently pervades the teaching of accountancy in our universities.

Absolution and Dispensation

At this point, I would normally be disposed to pointing a finger of shame at the FASB for the dignity it accorded what were clearly the sham transactions implicit in Statement 49, relating to Product-Financing Arrangements. But the passage of time has brought forth newer irritants; the most recent being the April 27, 1982, Exposure Draft of a "Proposed Statement of Financial Accounting Standards--Research and Development Arrangements."

The arrangements covered by the promulgation involve those where a high-technology enterprise (for example) contracts with a limited partnership whereby the latter would provide the funds to carry on R & D; the former would then have the right to acquire the "eurekas" for a stated sum, or royalty payout--in cash, stock and/or warrants.

In 34 discursive paragraphs--fitting for scholars in a theological seminary engaged in exegetic analysis--the distinguished Seven comprising the FASB came down flatly saying that sometimes the arrangement involves a liability, sometimes not--depending on the circumstances. In reaching this awesome, ambivalent conclusion, the Board was counselled by representatives from the major accounting firms, an attorney involved in hammering out these arrangements, representatives from brokerage firms which have been disseminating these limited partnership interests and, it should go without saying, from the leading high-technology firms involved in these arrangements. (Two members from the SEC staff, I am told, sat in as observers.)

And so once again the Board has demonstrated its naivete—the kind which led it into a cul-de-sac on leases, for example, leaving it to management and its astute lawyers, accountants and financial advisors to develop the contractual verbiage to permit the enterprise to perpetuate another layer of off-balance-sheet financing and off-the-books expenses. Did not the Board remember Memorex's "Proprietary Subsidiaries" which accomplished the identical objectives (then via "part purchase, part pooling")? Did not the Board learn from its Statement 49 experience? Obviously not: As Santayana observed, "We are destined to repeat the mistakes of history because we do not read it."

But my principal complaint is that the whole business does not call for a new standard. We have the good old traditional standard of "substance over form." Given that standard, all that needs to be said is that: Experience informs us that these arrangements should be presumed to be financing arrangements. However, this presumption may be overcome by a "preponderance of evidence" to the contrary.

And now, it should be noted, consistent with the FASB's proclivity for dispensing absolution and dispensation, the "standard" would not be applicable in any event to arrangements entered into before September 15, 1982.

Bravo for Storage Technology, et al.!

In the meantime, the Board is devoting enormous portions of its resources, both of time and money, to the pursuit of a chimera, namely, its Conceptual Framework Project.

My Indictment of the Conceptual Framework Project

I have seriously questioned FASB's Conceptual Framework Project. I have done so on several gounds, to wit:

1. The project implies that our profession is bereft of a body of knowledge worthy of the designation "a conceptual framework." I maintain that the writings over the past scores of years by Professors Paton, Littleton, Moontiz, Mautz, and others have provided us with an extraordinarily fine theoretical infrastructure.
2. I question the FASB's ability to articulate our derived body of knowledge with greater felicity of phrase and more inspired vision than those who have, heretofore, contributed to the shaping of our profession's body of knowledge.
3. The very existence of the FASB project has given it the excuse to avoid tackling such problems as business combinations,

"transient" preferred stock (i.e., preferred stock with mandatory redemption provisions).

4. The FASB in various promulgations of standards can be seen to be violating the precepts set forth in its concept statements. (For example, Statements 33 and 34 and 36.)

For all these reasons, I urge the Board to end this boondoggle and wasting of scarce resources, and to get on with the serious business—whatever that might be.

Our Profession's PR

Turning to the self-disciplinary process which prevails for our profession, we find the system of peer review which the SEC-Practice Section of the AICPA is presenting to the world as its deus ex machina. To the most limited extent to which I have been exposed to that process I am less than enchanted with it. Thus, as Sandy Burton put it, the firm on firm review smacks of the "mutual back scratching" syndrome. Further, while the review makes certain the i's are dotted and the t's are crossed, they fail to probe the behavioral environment which encourages, possibly even demands, that the critical judgment calls required of the partner in charge of the engagement somehow comform with the desires of the client's management.

But, in truth, I maintain that the SEC-Practice Section's hoopla about its PR keystone is essentially pretentious PR (here standing for public relations). Thus, I maintain that peer review is as old as accountancy is presumed to be a profession. We have always had a system of peer review by reason of our having a Code of Professional Ethics and a body to administer that Code. Further, I see peer review in adversary proceedings wherein one auditor discerns serious performance gaps by colleagues in our profession. I see it when academicians study the promulgations by independent auditors which demonstrate serious failures in GAAP and/or GAAS. So why does it seem as though the POB has discovered the wheel? Simply because the Ethics Division of the AICPA has, in fact, abdicated its fair responsibilities.

A Challenge to Accounting Academics

A most critical challenge confronting our colleagues in academe, relates to our research endeavor.

First, in this context, I shall consider what I believe to be acts of omission on our part. Thus, I find that our colleagues in academe are disinclined to pursue the in-depth analysis of a particular corporation or industry and to demonstrate the appropriateness or inappropriateness of the accounting policies and practices which were there impacted. It is true, there are far greater risks involved in this kind of research; the companies and accounting firms which were involved might take umbrage at our determinations and might even be sufficiently aroused as to bring an action for libel or an ethics complaint. But if we wish to go in swimming we must be prepared to get wet.

Granted, also, that the intrepidity of such a critical scholar might not be matched by a correspondingly intrepid editor or publisher. Further, the promotion, tenure or personnel and budget committees, or others in the administration of the scholar's institution, might look askance at such critical endeavors. So it is that the cost-benefit relationship resulting from this kind of investigative analysis might not be as advantageous as a more esoteric kind.

In so far as sins of omission are concerned, I am regularly distressed at observing the reams of scholarly output subsumed under the rubric "empirical research." It appears that some publications are committed to the dissemination of mathematical symbolism bordering on the occult; no one, I suspect, really understood what the symbols, ratios, equations, formulas and/or curves are supposed to present. Nonetheless, because the publications would then be presumed to represent profound scientific scholarship, the ostensibly scholarly output is published.

I regularly inquire of my more scholarly colleagues precisely what relevance their research may have had for the balance sheet or income statement or accounting principles and practices. The responses are essentially, "What is a balance sheet, what is an income statement, what are accounting principles and practices?"

I urge my colleagues in academe to take the lead in casting off the shackles of authoritarianism imposed on the profession by the FASB and the Accounting Establishment generally. To this end, I urge that we make clear that the intellectual, the conceptual infrastructure of our profession is much too complex, much too advanced to permit it to be determined by seven mortals, no matter how brilliant they may be. There is no other professional pursuit which professes as advanced and advancing body of knowledge which has abdicated the responsibility for establishing that body of knowledge to an authoritarian (sometimes seen as a totalitarian) body.

The SEC—RIP

Moving along to the Securities and Exchange Commission, how nostalgically I think back to the era which I dubbed that of the three S's, i.e., Commissioner A. A. Sommer, Stanley Sporkin, and Sandy Burton. What a time of hope and promise there was that our financial reporting process would, in fact, be moved forward towards full and fair disclosures.

Alas, we do have a couple of S's now--in the persons of Chairman Shad and Chief Accountant Sampson. I am certain these gentlemen will not take umbrage by my observing that their world is about 180 degrees at variance from that of the three S's.

Specifically, for a score of years I have conducted studies, written and lectured on various aspects of the management advisory services-independence of the auditor controversy. I am convinced by the preponderance of evidence developed by my research and that of other academicians that the concurrent rendering of MAS by the firm performing the ostensibly independent audit function detracts from the statement user's perception of the auditor's independence. Even the Accounting Establishment (as represented, say, by its Public Oversight Board) is constrained to concur in this conclusion.

I have gone further and demonstrated, at least to my satisfaction, that the rendering of the nexus of services concurrently has, actually, detracted from such independence.

As a result of the pressures from several academic studies, and especially from the Congress (i.e., the Moss and Metcalf Committees), the SEC promulgated Accounting Series Releases 250 and 264.

The former, as we are undoubtedly aware, merely called for the disclosure in proxy material of the fee proportions derived from the peripheral services where such fees exceeded a specified tolerance; the latter ASR was, essentially a philosophic discourse on the conflicts which may be inherent in the duality or multiplicity of function. In short, there was nothing in those promulgations which asserted "thou shalt not!"

But then, with the advent of the Shad Administration, the Accounting Establishment determined that it had the "friend in court" to eradicate these promulgations. And so it was that in a matter of months the registrants were no longer required to disclose the potentially contaminating relationships--the independent auditor was put on his "scout's oath" to "do right."

What I find particularly irksome is the arrogance or presumptuousness on the part of our colleagues. They assert that there is no conflict--and that anyone who does see one is paranoid. That may well be true but: These same accountants then maintain that they will not divulge the factual circumstances required to permit others who might be interested to make a concurring or contrary determination.

Surely, our colleagues would not permit such a privilege to "work both sides of the street" to members of the bar (especially the judiciary), members of the President's Cabinet (n.b., the debate surrounding William French Smith), members of boards of directors (nepotistic or other potentially conflicting relationships are required to be disclosed). Why should accountants be presumed to be possessed of higher standards of selflessness or integrity than these other pursuits? The only answer is that we have been able to get away with it--and the SEC is aiding and abetting our endeavors which, under the circumstances, I consider to be insidious.

There is yet another manifestation of the determination

of the Commission to relax its responsibility for assuring the effectiveness of the independent audit process. Five years ago, in the course of its testimony before the Metcalf Committee of the United States Senate, the Commission agreed to submit an annual report to the Congress on the "Accounting Profession and the Commission's Oversight Role."

Pursuant to this undertaking, reports were promulgated in mid-year 1978, 1979 and 1980. Alas, with the new Administration the covenant was broken--there were no reports for 1981, and I do not expect one this year.

A Plea for Euthanasia

In this mood, I took the occasion several months ago to write to Congressman John Dingell, Chairman of the U.S. House of Representatives' Committee on Energy and Commerce, urging that he schedule hearings of his Subcommittee on Oversight and Investigations into the present direction of the SEC. I then suggested, with sincere sadness, that unless a reversal in that trend could be effected, the Congress might consider aborting the SEC. I would then have the Congress proclaim that the traditional rule of caveat emptor is back in the saddle and is riding Wall Street. In short, the prevailing environment is little short of a hoax. My views in this regard were quoted in an April 19th article in the U.S. News & World Report.

The Courts on Trial

Moving along now to the courts.

"Getting Government Off Our Backs" may have been the winning battle cry of the 1980 Presidential elections; actually, the Government was being taken off the backs of corporate enterprise at least as far back as 1976 by successive decisions of the Supreme Court of the United States. Most certainly, we in the accounting profession might well have discerned that tendency (and even rejoiced in it) when the Supreme Court of the United States in Ernst & Ernst v. Hochfelder set back the administration of our Securities Laws by some two-score years.

The Supreme Court's First Strike: Hochfelder

The majority opinion of the Court stated the issue at the outset (it should be noted that Ernst & Ernst, the auditors, were the defendant-petitioners; Hochfelder the euchred plaintiff-respondent):

> The issue in this case is whether an action for civil damages may be under Sec. 10(b) of the Securities Exchange Act of 1934. . .and Securities and Exchange Commission Rule 10b-5 . . . in the absence of an allegation of intent to deceive, manipulate or defraud on the part of the defendant.

After an exhaustive analysis of the semantics of the 1934 congressional enactment, the court decreed that " . . . the language of Section 10(b). . .clearly connotes intentional misconduct . . ." Since there were no allegations made that Ernst & Ernst were accomplices of the perpetrator of the fraud against Hochfelder, et al., they were exculpated. The language of the decision would appear to require a direct involvement or conspiracy on the part of the auditors to support an action under Rule 10b-5. The majority's decision was put into clear perspective by the opening paragraph of a sharply worded dissent by Justice Blackmun:

> Once again . . . the court interprets Sec. 10(b) . . . restrictively and narrowly and thereby stultifies recovery for the victim. This time the Court does so by confining the Rule to situations where the defendant has "scienter," that is, the intent to deceive, manipulate, or defraud." Sheer negligence, the Court says, is not within the reach of the statute and the Rule, and was not contemplated when the great reforms of 1933, 1934, and 1942 were effectuated by Congressional Commission.

Blackmun's dissent includes an impassioned plea for holding the auditors responsible for their apparently conceded negligence, pointing up the critical role played by the auditor-accountants in the securities arena.

Nevertheless, the Court has decreed that negligence by a professional person is not sufficient to hold him liable under the anti-fraud provision of the Securities Laws to third parties victimized by his negligence, even though the person claims competence, expertise, and responsibility. For me this pretentious claim is a fraud if negligence is a hidden factor in the profession's tool box. To make matters even more confusing, there are those legal experts who are asserting that even reckless negligence would not support an action against an auditor under 10(b).

Strike Two: Redington

Then, in June, 1979, the Supreme Court dropped the second shoe--its decision in Touche Ross & Co. v. Edward S. Redington (442 U.S. 560).

Justice Rehnquist's opener (in the opinion written on behalf of himself and six of his colleagues) was as follows:

> Once again, we are called upon to decide whether a private remedy is implicit in a statute not expressly providing one . . . Here we decide whether customers of securities brokerage firms that are required to file certain financial reports with regulatory authorities by Section 17(a) of the Securities Exchange Act of 1934 have an implied cause of action for damages under Section 17(a) against who audit such reports based on misstatements contained in the reports.

The case arose from the fact that Weis Securities, Inc., a registered broker-dealer, went "belly up" in 1973. Edward Redington was designated as the trustee in liquidation, whereupon he instituted suit against Touche Ross for the benefit of the Securities Investors Protection Corporation (SIPC), which had provided the funds to discharge Weis's liability to its customers as required by the act which created SIPC.

Touche Ross, as Weis' auditors, had prepared for filing

with the SEC the annual reports on Weis' financial condition, as required by Section 17(a) of the Securities Exchange Act of 1934. The theory of the plaintiffs' case was essentially that proper audits by Touche would have revealed Weis' difficulties at an earlier stage--permitting "remedial action to forestall liquidation or to lessen the adverse financial consequences of such liquidation to Weis customers," and that Section 17(a) gave rise to an implied right of action against Touche to recoup customer losses which could have been prevented.

The Court rejected Redington's theory that 17(a) gave rise to a private cause of action against the auditors; instead, according to the majority:

> . . . Section 17(a) simply requires broker-dealers and others to keep such records and file such reports as the (Securities and Exchange) Commission may prescribe. It does not, by its terms, purport to create a private cause of action in favor of anyone . . .
>
> The intent of Section 17(a) is evident from its face. Section 17(a) is like provisions in countless other statutes that simply require certain regulated businesses to keep and file periodic reports to enable the relevant governmental authorities to perform their regulatory functions.
>
> . . . The information contained in the Section 17(a) reports is intended to provide the Commission, the Exchange and other authorities with a sufficiently early warning to enable them to take appropriate action to protect investors before the financial collapse of the particular broker-dealer involved. But Section 17(a) does not by any stretch of its language purport to

> confer private damage rights or, indeed, any remedy in the event the regulatory authorities are unsuccessful in achieving their objectives and the broker becomes insolvent before corrective steps can be taken.

Justice Marshall, as the lone dissenter, lamented the majority's view, asserting " . . . Because the SEC lacks the resources to audit all the documents that brokers file, it must rely on certification by accountants . . . Implying a private right to action would both facilitate the SEC's enforcement efforts and provide an incentive for accountants to perform the certification functions properly."

Hochfelder left open the question as to whether the scienter standard was required to be met by the SEC when it sought injunctive relief against someone who is alleged to have violated the antifraud provisions of the Securities Laws. In fact, in deciding SEC v. Arthur Young & Co. in litigation arising out of the collapse of the Goetek oil ventures, the courts (Federal, District, and Circuit) presumed (without resolving) that the Commission need prove mere negligence, i.e., scienter. (The courts held for AY on the ground that the firm had complied with generally accepted auditing standards.)

The Third Strike: Aaron

The High Court's Third Strike: On June 2, 1980, the Supreme Court of the United States, decided the so-called Aaron case against the SEC insofar as Rule 10(b)-5 is concerned. The case involved a broker-dealer in securities. After a strict linguistic exegetic analysis of the statutory provision worthy of the medieval scholastics, the Court decreed that the Commission had to meet the Hochfelder standard, just like an ordinary private citizen.

There was a dissent on this issue by Mr. Justice Blackmun (joined by Justices Brennan and Marshall); nevertheless, by the 6 to 3 majority the Court further rendered impotent the Securities and Exchange Commission in its endeavors to exorcise deceptive practices from the securities market place.

I would be less distressed by these judicial developments if I were of the view that our profession had, in fact, compensated for the judicial turnabout by an effective process of self-discipline. But, as I have pointed up previously in this presentation, the circumstances are otherwise—the self-regulatory apparatus may be in place but it is certainly not functioning effectively.

The Congress of the United States—Sleeping Giant Again?

Two years ago when addressing the Congress of Accounting Historians in London on the subject of "The Congressional Oversight of the Accounting Profession in the United States," I observed that for more than two score years after the enactment of the Securities Acts of 1933 and 1934 the Congress treated the profession with benign neglect. I made this sweeping observation after a reasonably complete search by the Library of Congress of any pronouncements by the legislature relating to accountancy as a profession or its responsibilities under the Securities Laws. There were, of course, references to accountancy as an incident to public utility regulation or taxation—but insofar as the audit responsibility was concerned the Congress could not care less—or so it seemed.

But then the years 1976-1979 (especially the first two of those years) were different. Thus, 1976 witnessed the hearings by the Subcommittee on Oversight and Investigations of the U.S. House of Representatives' Committee on Interstate and Foreign Commerce (the "Moss Committee"). During the following year, the Subcommittee on Reports, Accounting and Management of the U.S. Senate's Committee on Governmental Operations (the "Metcalf Committee") promulgated a staff study entitled _The Accounting Establishment;_ that publication, in turn, served as the basis for extensive hearings during the spring and summer of that year, leading to a November, 1977, report from the Committee. That report set forth a series of recommendations for, and expectations of, the profession.

There were some further hearings in early 1978 (by the Moss Committee) and 1979 (by the Eagleton Committee, which inherited the responsibility on the death of Senator Metcalf).

Be it remembered that a half dozen years ago the Congress was jolted by, inter alia, Corporate "Watergating," Equity Funding, Penn Central, National Student Marketing. This series of accounting fiascos is undoubtedly exceeded in amount and implications by, again inter alia, Penn Square, Drysdale, Citicorp and Chase internal control failures, Datapoint, McCormick. Thus, the climate is right for the Congress, like the fictional sleeping giant, to be reawakened from its slumbers. It is to that end, as noted, that I wrote to the Subcommittee on Oversight and Investigation of the House of Representatives' Committee on Commerce and Energy--the investigative body that stated it all a half dozen years ago.

Quo Vadis?

In view of my misgivings regarding the prevailing practices governing the independent, external audit, where shall we turn, how shall we proceed? I propose two, essentially diametrically opposed, alternatives to the profession's leadership; essentially my plea is consistent with Deuteronomy where, we are enjoined, "I have set before you good and evil therefore choose life so that you and your seed might live."

Thus, I would first urge that the profession take to heart the great expectations which society has for the independent auditor in the fulfillment of his responsibility in the arena of publicly-owned corporations. In this connection regarding our generally accepted auditing standards I would move to emancipate our colleagues in practice to determine the alternatives which they believe to be appropriate under varying circumstances. I would then insist that the auditor, here presumed to be really independent and intrepid, apply the particular alternative which he believes to be uniquely appropriate--and to assume the responsibility for that determination with all of his professional credentials "on the line."

I would expect the auditor to be prepared to justify his judgment calls and to make clear the reasons why he believed those for which he opted were, in his view, optimal. While criticism of the auditor's determination might be expected from his colleagues in practice, and even more from our colleagues in academe, I would avoid second guessing or "Monday-morning quarterbacking." Thus, full faith and credit should be afforded the auditor's judgments if they were made after full and careful deliberation and without let or hindrance from the client or others in the accounting firm's hierarchy. In short, the process of peer review in the judicial system or of those who pursue the writing of history should be implemented for our profession.

So it is that I would expect to find a continuous

interrelationship and feedback between theoretical research and practice; I would expect the relationship to be one of tension and friction, but above all, symbiotic.

It should be noted that the "emancipation proclamation" implies a quantum leap or "revolutionary reversal" in the prevailing relationship between the auditor and the financial statements which he has certified.

No longer should the auditor be afforded the luxury of shrugging off the application of a less-than-optimal accounting alternative by asserting that the statements are those of management and not his. My proposal would put an end to what I call the "greshamizing of GAAP"—a process whereby an accounting alternative is deemed permissible, however far-fetched, if the client or the auditor can locate it buried somewhere in the bowels of the NARS.

As an incident to this fulfillment, I would insist that the independent auditor undertake the responsibility presumed to have been vested in him by the Foreign Corrupt Practices Act of 1977. This would imply that he undertake a direct and absolute study of the corporation's internal control system; by the phrase "direct and absolute" I intend an invidious distinction from the prevailing norm, whereby the review is undertaken only as an incident to satisfying the auditor regarding the reliability of the records as the medium for the financial statements.

Also as an incident to this fulfillment I would expect the independent auditor to review the composition and effectiveness of the entity's independent audit committee of the board of directors. As a guide to this review, the auditor should comprehend the role of the committee as envisaged by the American Law Institute in its recently proposed "Restatement and Recommendations: Principles of Corporate Governance and Structure."

Should the profession fail to respond effectively to this challenge or, having responded, finds itself incapable of fulfilling the role expected of it by society, then I recommend that we eliminate the requirement for the so-called independent, external audit and proclaim to society that the traditional standard of caveat emptor is once again in vogue. We would, at least, be proceeding with dignity and integrity, we would be exorcising the myth, the hoax, under which society is presently laboring.

This proposal for an exorcism might be seen to complement the suggestion made above for aborting the Securities and Exchange Commission should it proceed on its present course.

It should be reemphasized that the proposals for the exorcism and abortion are not being made here lightly, as a flip, idle threat. Instead, these proposals come from my appraisal, all too frequently an agonizing reappraisal, of the prevailing environment of corporate accounting and accountability.

While there is yet some time available to the profession, while we still have an important reservoir of confidence and credibility with the public generally, I urge that "we choose life so that we and our seed might live."

APPENDIX A

REPORT FROM MANAGEMENT

GENERAL ELECTRIC CORPORATION

ANNUAL REPORT - 1981

To Share Owners of General Electric Company

The financial statements of General Electric Company and consolidated affiliates are presented on pages 39 through 50 of this Annual Report. These statements have been prepared by management and are in conformity with generally accepted accounting principles appropriate in the circumstances. The statements include amounts that are based on our best estimates and judgments. Financial information elsewhere in this Annual Report is consistent with that in the financial statements.

General Electric maintains a strong system of internal financial controls and procedures, supported by a staff of corporate auditors and supplemented by resident auditors located around the world. This system is designed to provide reasonable assurance, at appropriate cost, that assets are safeguarded and that transactions are executed in accordance with management's authorization, and are recorded and reported properly. The system is time tested, innovative and responsive to change. Perhaps the most important safeguard in this system is the fact that the Company has long emphasized the selection, training and development of professional financial managers to implement and oversee the proper application of its internal controls and the reporting of management's stewardship of corporate assets and maintenance of accounts in conformity with generally accepted accounting principles.

The independent public accountants

provide an objective independent review as to management's discharge of its responsibilities insofar as they relate to the fairness of reported operating results and financial condition. They obtain and maintain an understanding of GE accounting and financial policies and controls, and conduct such tests and related procedures as they consider necessary to arrive at an opinion on the fairness of financial statements. The Audit Committee of the Board of Directors, which is composed solely of Directors from outside the Company, maintains an ongoing appraisal of the effectiveness of audits and the independence of the public accountants. The Committee meets periodically with the public accountants, management and internal auditors to review the work of each. The public accountants have free access to the Committee, without management present, to discuss the results of their audit work and their opinions on the adequacy of internal financial controls and the quality of financial reporting. The Committee also reviews the Company's accounting policies, internal accounting controls, and the Annual Report and proxy material.

Management has long recognized its responsibility for conducting the Company's affairs in an ethical and socially responsible manner. The commitment to this responsibility is reflected in key written policy statements covering, among other subjects, potentially conflicting outside business interests of employees, compliance with antitrust laws, and proper conduct of domestic and international business practices. Ongoing educational, communication and review programs are designed to create a strong compliance environment and to make it clearly understood that deviation from Company policies will not be tolerated.

APPENDIX B

THE LOCKHEED AIRBUS(T) SAGA

The 1981 report of the Lockheed Aircraft Corporation stepped down its L-1011 TriStar Program to Discontinued Operations. The decision, we are told, was the consequence of a "lack of orders." We were informed that the company has booked orders for 244 TriStars, of which 220 had been delivered.

In my 1976-book, More Debits Than Credits, I dubbed that target "pie in the sky" and asserted that the half-billion dollar pool of costs (carried as a current asset, no less) should be drastically written down. Shortly after that writing, in my testimony on May 22, 1976, before the Subcommittee on Oversight and Investigations of the U.S. House of Representatives Committee on Interstate and Foreign Commerce, I stated:

> I move to the matter which to my mind is so critically symptomatic of the burdens that I see confronting the accounting profession presently. First . . . I despair at . . . what is going on in the case of the Lockheed Corp. accountings. I despair there because . . . so much of what is wrong with that company's accountings is visible, is discernible--is discernible by the Securities and Exchange Commission, is discernible by the General Accounting Office . . . . It appears to me. . . that the SEC and GAO are almost determined to shut their eyes to what it is that management and their auditors are doing. So it is that I make clear that there is a half billion dollars

> on the corporation's balance sheet among its assets which is not worth the erasure to wipe it off the balance sheet . . . .

Now, as of the end of 1981, Lockheed wrote off about $400 million after tax (representing $730 million pretax which was theretofore embedded among its assets). Before all this gets washed up in history let me recapitulate some of the background facts of this ill-starred program.

What gave rise to my crie de coeur? Briefly, Lockheed was accounting for the L-1011s on the basis of the so-called program method; each plane in the program (300 were envisaged at the time of my writing and testifying) was to be assigned a presumed average cost—regardless of the actual costs which were incurred in its production. Any costs incurred in excess of the assigned costs would be deferred until the learning curve would turn to a favorable slope so that subsequent incurred costs on a particular plane would be less than the average--thereby permitting an absorption of the previously deferred costs.

This is all well and good, at least conceptually. The program method could be seen to be consistent with the percentage-of-completion method for profit recognition. The critical flaw in the Lockheed calculus was that the incremental costs per plane were destined to exceed the incremental revenues. Given that condition, just how the company hoped to absorb the half-billion blob which prevailed in late 1975 should have boggled the mind of any reasonable observer.

The Accounting Establishment "Refutes" Briloff:

What followed in the wake of my writing and testimony?

First, in October, 1976, the then FASB Chairman Marshall Armstrong wrote to Congressman John E. Moss, the Chairman of the House Committee, commenting most acerbically on my presentation (and the Committee's reliance thereon).

Second, when Arthur Young & Company testified before the Metcalf Committee in mid-1977, the firm went to great lengths to refute Briloff's allegations. The firm persisted in asserting that Lockheed was, in fact, enjoying a positive contribution to margin from its TriStars.

To this I responded by citing Lockheed's published data demonstrating that through 1976 there was a negative incremental margin on the L-1011 Program. Arthur Young never responded to my condemnation of its statements before the Senate committee.

Third, starting with late 1975, Lockheed did proceed to "bite the bullet"--but this it did on the installment plan, i.e., by writing off the blob at the rate of $50 million annually.

But the Figures Do Not Lie (Eventually):

And what has been the record of that program? From the annual reports losses were incurred in the following staggering amounts (in $ million):

1975	$ 94
1976	$125
1977	$120
1978	$119
1979	$188
1980	$199
1981	$129
Total	$974

These dismal results notwithstanding, the company and its independent auditors persisted in their contention that the hundreds of millions of dollars of deferred costs were properly to be booked as assets.

I have in various previous writings quoted the full text of the CPA rhetoric with which the CPA's made their presentations and have alluded to this rhetoric as pettifoggery. If any of you have a sardonic sense of humor I suggest you read the litany. You will then recognize the reasons for my saying, "It hurts when I laugh."

And so this long saga is brought to an end and Lockheed's bookkeeping agonies will be naught but a footnote to history. Before it does so, however, let me add one final note—a note of sadness and cynicism.

According to the company's 1981 report, Lockheed was compelled to implement a quasi-reorganization as of year end.

This involved the shifting of $62 million from the preferred stock account to "additional capital," and restated the carrying value of certain investment properties, producing another credit to "additional capital" of $33 million--thereby creating an additional common shareholders' equity of $95 million. The company then "zeroed out" its $116 million deficit in retained earnings by a transfer to the additional capital account. This, then, gives Lockheed a fresh start in so far as its retained earnings account is concerned.

After completing this process of "artificial respiration," Lockheed's entire shareholder' equity (preferred and common) aggregated $141 million; its income from continuing operations for the year amounted to $154 million. Clearly, absent these 1981 earnings Lockheed could not have scraped together enough credit to avoid an actual deficit in shareholders' equity. So it is, according to my hypothesis, that Lockheed was permitted by its auditors to perpetuate debits on its balance sheet as specious assets until the critical objective had been attained—that happened during 1981.

Sic transit gloria mundi!

Discussion

OF

DOUBLE ENTRY: DOUBLE THINK: DOUBLE SPEAK

PARTICIPANTS IN THE DISCUSSION

OF

ABRAHAM BRILLOF'S

PAPER

Martin Bennis, Baruch College, City University of New York

Maria L. Bullen, Georgia State University

Allan Cherry, Loyola Mary Mount University

Jeffrey Harkins, University of Idaho

Charles Lindblom, Yale University

Discussion introduced by Professor Briloff:

ABRAHAM BRILOFF:

Those who have given thought to the professional responsibility and professional commitment to society must be concerned with the current emphasis and obsession of large audit firms with growth and the retention of the client rather then the commitment to the fulfillment of the profession's transcendent responsibilities. Coupled with the fact that there has occurred, within the accounting firms, low balling with respect to the audit fees. This has had several results: First, it produced enormous pressures on the auditing staff to either cut corners with respect to the audit program, or to sign up for things that were not in fact done. So that, in the first instance, this self-cannibalization puts a heavy price on those involved in the audit responsibility, either in terms of time pressures, or scheduling pressures.

Second, these firms hope to make up part of the losses that they are sustaining by low-bidding (or the low balling on the audit work) through the increasing financial benefits of non-audit work: The management advisory services' role which—as I see it—contaminates the independent audit function. In other words, the one becomes the entree into the other. This is probably the consequence of identifying with the philosophical proclivities of major clients on the part of the major accounting firms, and possibly accountants quite generally. And so, as a consequence, in their testifying before the Congress, the accounting firms sincerely see things consistent with the way in which the corporate management see things because there is a certain consistency in terms of their income level, their objectives, their political philosophies, and economic philosophies.

I have very severe misgivings with the book: The Big Eight, by Mark Stevens. But yet one dimension comes through very directly; and that is that so much of the major firms' activities are committed to the PR and the hard sell aspects (against the pursuit of truth) that it could be considered to be the entire professional implications of our pursuit.

QUESTIONER:

Why do you suppose that persons who have suffered losses in security transactions due to what could be construed as misinformation, and attorneys who represent the interests of those who have suffered losses, attack the independence of the profession as the basis for a case?

ABRAHAM BRILOFF:

I do not know whether your premise is necessarily the case. I must assume, for example, the Arthur Andersen situation, with respect to the Fund of Funds, that the plaintiff demonstrated that the accountants did sacrifice their independence in going along with the fake valuation that was put on the property by their client; and thus they failed to demonstrate their own independent judgment with respect to what was being done. I do not know specifically what it is that you might have in mind when you speak of attacking the independence of the profession. It would appear to me that we demonstrate lack of independence if we show that the auditors saw serious failures--let us say in the internal control system--but nevertheless determined to play shut-eye because, to raise the issue might prove embarrassing, possibly to themselves in not having discovered it in the year or two previously; or embarrassing to the client because, if they blew the whistle, then it might be that the entire situation might blow up in their faces. Most certainly, ignoring a deterioration in the internal control aspects is, as I would see it, a manifestation of a loss of independence. Certainly a loss of independent judgment.

So it is that the demonstration of a lack of independence can come forth in many different ways. In fact, I would say that, implicit in recent court decisions is that if the auditor knew of reckless negligence and failed to find that out, he is liable. My own presumption is that if the auditor knew that the situation is perverted and did not respond to it, that, to my mind, implies a breakdown in the auditing field.

If, however, what you mean is: Have they demonstrated, in any particular case, that the independence may have been contaminated by the performance of the management advisory services (MAS) and, as a result, the MAS produced a certain end result which affected the audit, it may very well be that they just did not have to go that far with the respect to the trail. However, I must say that, when I was working with counsel, I did ask counsel to obtain the billing record of an accounting firm to see what other services were being rendered, and we did get some rather interesting disclosures. The case was settled very quickly.

QUESTIONER:

Given your comments, which I agree with whole-heartedly, about the FASB and their failures and trivializations, and given the SEC's current failure through their move toward deregulations, what direction do you think we can turn to, if any, for an option for standard setting in the Paton and Littleton sense? I am really at a loss at this one.

ABRAHAM BRILOFF:

Do not be at a loss. My first recommendation to the Financial Accounting Standard Board, which has been in existence now from 1973 to, let us say, 1982, which is nine years, is that it is time for them to take a sabbatical, and just rest, and in effect to say, "You know, we have an extraordinary fine set of standards. We have an extraordinary fine conceptual framework which has evolved over time. What we need are not new principles of accounting; what we need are better principles for the accountants. Give us a chance now to do the job which we know needs to be done." And then for us, not to move with vengeance, but instead, for us as academicians, to now exercise our prerogatives that we will retain our independence of outlook without let or hindrance. We will study financial reports that come forth, to determine whether that which was done, was consistent with the best of our accounting precepts as we see them, and we will not accept as a response from the certifying accountant that, "Our task is not to determine the fairness of the financial statements, ours is merely to determine whether, somehow or other, they conform to generally accepted accounting principles." We will not accept that kind of a rationalization from them. We will say to them, just as we presume that colleagues in the medical profession might say to their colleagues if they were doing their task in clear review, "Don't tell us that which you did, might somehow or other be rationalized. We want to know whether you did that which was the best consistent with the state of the art and the science at present." If the independent accountant says that I made those judgments based upon these views and these circumstances that prevail, and this is what I consider to be best on the basis of my judgment, I will not second-guess him. I will engage him in dialogue. But I will not accept the "greshamizing" response that, "I merely determine whether that which was done can, somehow or other, be subsumed in GAPP."

This is where I would like to see our colleagues in academe go. Instead, our colleagues, all to often, are encouraged to move into an esoteric abstraction of developing a statistical configuration with models and the like, and they do not know what it is that they are after. The editors surely do not know, but they are too embarrassed to reject it because of the fact that then they would be disclosing their ignorance. Just look at the Accounting Review. If you ask your colleagues, "Tell me how, after years of effort on your part, how these promulgations impact on a balance sheet or the income statement," their response might be, "What is a balance sheet? What is an income statement?" Am I being facetious? Yes, but only in part. But there is the kind of accounting "research" which will find very heavy subsidization from Big Eight accounting firms, or from the Institute.

It is not easy to study those footnotes. It is not easy to come out controversially and to say, "In this particular context we believe you have fouled the nest." It is not easy to write about Safeguard, for example, as I did a year ago, and then to receive some highly inflammatory commentary in the form of letters to the shareholders from the chairman of the corporation. It is not easy to face up to litigation and the depositions, even though you prevail. But yet, if you want to go in swimming, you have to be prepared to get wet. The challenge is there, and if it is not for us in academe, then for whom? Can we leave it to the personnel in the major accounting firms? This is another grievance I have about the organizational structure of the firms. Conformity is one of the demands and requirements put upon them, and dissent is not particularly encouraged, certainly not if you want to make partners, and that, of course, is the sine qua non of the accountants' aspirations.

QUESTIONER:

I have done some financial statements reviews but not on your scale. Do you not think the academics in your proposal could do an even better job if they had access to working papers and things like this? I will not state what an audit committee's intent is, but it seems that most of the people on the committee are buddies or the friends of friends with the people who are in charge of the corporation. They might put one person on there who they have gotten through the grapevine or somebody who is recognized as being a liberal or something or else.

ABRAHAM BRILOFF:

There is no question but I must respond in the affirmative to what is being suggested. Yet while we, as independent auditors, recognize a third party responsibility, we hold zealously to the concept of confidentiality with respect to our relationships with our clients. So much so that this is held almost inviolate, even in the face of the litigation as we have had in certain areas of taxation. Even the Securities and Exchange Commission could not get the Public Oversight Board and the Divisional for Firms to budge on the peer review to see the record papers so that we can judge for ourselves how effective this was done.

I must admit that I have had some lucky breaks on that score. With access to records, we could do a more effective job, but absent that, let us do the best that we can and exercise our independent judgment with respect to the product that we see.

QUESTIONER:

I am curious about the view that you have about getting the job done. If I go to a doctor and say, "I think that I have an ailment, or something is bothering me," he does not apply an elaborate set of rules and say, "yes" or "no." That is, he pokes around and he says, "maybe." "Maybe you do, you cannot be sure. We could do a lot more work to find out, and it is probably not worth it." I might reply to him, "Look, you are talking about my health, my life, it is important. I want to know: Have I got an ailment or not?" And he says, "I still do not know. You can live with that uncertainty, there are different courses of action you can take to cope with that." You do not really have to know. Suppose I were President of the United States, and I called an economist and said, "Is business going to get better or worse in the next six months?" An economist would apply the rules and come up with several possible answers: "It might get better, it might get worse." The President of the United States might reply that he had to know these things. But the economist says, "No, you do not. The world is uncertain; what you have to know is what these uncertainties are." Tell him to go to an accountant and say, "I run this firm, I want to know if I made any money last year." Your people seem to buy into responsibility to give an answer, and to sweat your lives out developing sets of rules, so that you will come to definitive, precise and unique answers. But since, in complex business activity, one never can tell until some years after, whether you really made any money, or whether your net worth really went up that year or went down, the uniqueness and precision of the answer is false, and you are giving perhaps the manager of the business information he does not really need to have. All he really needs to know are the range of possibilities and the alternative courses of action to deal with that.

You are engaged in the kind of task of scientific observation. The complex business institution is saying something about its health or its prospects, and in no other area of scientific observation of the natural order or the social world does anyone accept such an extraordinary responsibility for precise and unique answers. Now, maybe I do not understand why you do it. Perhaps you do something very unusual in the profession for which I do not see specific justification in the long run. In the short run, I can see that the law requires the use of accounting data. But the law can be changed. Why do you do what you do?

ABRAHAM BRILOFF:

Let me press this point. By giving you a story that is apocryphal--but ironically I really meant it to be a particularly appropriate response--and then respond in a somewhat more formal way. The way in which I introduced my book, Unaccountable Accounting, is anecdotal about the owner of a closely held business that determined to go public and present his financial statements to an underwriting firm to review, to determine whether the firm would be prepared to take the securities to the marketplace. The underwriting firm said, "You have an extraordinary fine business here; by all means I want to take it public and to sell the securities to the public. However, in order to give a certain sense of dignity and prestige to these statements, we really have to get a different auditor, because while your auditor is a fine local firm that is as honest as can be, and we have no question about that which he has presented is the ultimate of integrity, yet we need one of the Big Eight accounting firms to sign up." The owner said, "Well what's the Big Eight, how do you spell it: e-i-g-h-t, or is it a-t-e?" The owner then asked, "Which one shall I turn to?" The underwriter said, "You are going to make the determination. Remember, once you select one you are going to have to live with that firm for long periods of time." The owner went back to his office, and the next day he called the underwriter and said, "I have got it, I am going to opt for one of the Eight." And the underwriter said, "What did you do, spin the bottle or something of that sort?" "No," he replied, "I did it all very scientifically." "But what do you mean by scientifically?" "Well, I called in the partners one after the other, and I said to them, "What does two-plus-two equal?" And each one said, "Four," excepting that lucky Arthur who looked at me, stroked his chin and said, "Sir, what number do you have in mind?"

Now the story is somewhat apocryphal, but not entirely. It may not have been one of the Arthurs, it may have been one of the Petes. Forgive me for saying so: Your question is really derivative from your lack of awareness as to what we mean by the accounting determinations in generally accepted accounting principles. There is a broad set of alternatives and options that might be used, and this is true even though part of the myth that we perpetrate on the public is that we come forth with debits precisely equaling credits. And I must admit, here and now, and I confess that no matter how many statements I have studied, excepting typographical aberrations, I have never seen one where the debits do not equal the credits. Now, this is part of the myth that we are perpetuating through the very appearance of precision. It is just like a reading of blood pressure or an EKG. The very appearance of precision is part of the hoax that we are perpetrating. The only point I am making is (and here I come back very specifically to your hypothetical question), that when I turn to the doctor and he has examined me, I do not want him then to turn on me and say, "Tell me what the diagnosis should be." This is precisely what occurs when corporate management turns to the independent auditor to examine the determinations that were made by management.

With respect to the subsidiary question that you raised about the President of the United States who presently, at least, must be turning to whatever economists would give the answer that the President has in mind. It must be because of the fact that he is getting this counsel that we are really in a most felicitous economic state. While there are economists around giving such advice to him, other economists have some serious misgivings. The point is that, with respect to these really close decisions that management requires for the conduct of its own affairs, management has on the entity's own internal staff, accountants, who are far more knowledgeable of the numbers and the operational implications and ramifications of that corporation's decision-making than the outside auditor even cares about, so that decision making by management is generally not predicated on what the auditor will be determining, excepting that management might say, "Now if we structure the take-over in this fashion, how will it look on the financial statements?" And the auditor will say, "If you do it this way, it will have a positive effect; if you do it the other way, it will have an inimical effect." Which way do you want to have it?" "Are you so rich that you want to have an adverse effect?" So in that way we do effect the decision-making process.

QUESTIONER:

You are talking about the management bias in these unique answers you get, and because there are so many different biases, how can there be a different unique answer without the bias. It might pick up somebody else's bias, but you are still working with bias. What I want to get at is not the character of the bias or its existence (I can see all you say there), but this interesting question as to why you want the unique answer. Why are you not interested in freeing yourself from constraints that seem to impose on you, as on no other group in society, a responsibility for a unique answer? Now the most obvious answer I suppose is, "Well, people and institutions are going to be taxed, and you have to have unique answers to decide what their tax vulnerability is." Under existing law, perhaps that is true, but you can easily imagine changes in law that would give the taxing authority a hard-to-make discretionary judgment of the tax accountability, the same way that there is a quite discretionary judgment about the value of my house when you impose a property tax on it. So in the long run, it seems to me the profession would want to work toward opinions on the range of possibilities and the qualifications in saying, "This is your net worth." Or, "This is your income for the year." Or, "This is your degree of loss," and break away from what I gather is a deeply established sense of obligation to try to bring it all down to one unique statement.

ABRAHAM BRILOFF:

Actually, we are not unique in terms of the necessity to make unique determinations. When, for example, I go to buy an insurance policy from a particular firm, I am presented with a certain number as being the premium I have to pay. Someone, somehow or another, has taken from an enormous mass of numbers and regulatory determinants, a certain figure that falls out as being my premium. Someone has made a unique decision. In the case of accountancy, for various understandable reasons, we have been committed setting forth determinations in numerical terms. The mistake might very well be, in our making the public feel that when we come forth with a number that is engraved in stone, and this is part of what it is that I am saying that the public must understand. Now, when the public understands that this is the result of a sincere and intense appraisal on our part of all the factors and determinants that entered into the situation, all mass of transactions, the legal framework in which the transactions took place, and the reality and substance of it; this is the best number that we--with our professional independence--came forth as being the definitive answer. Just as with an appraisal, whether it be with your house or with respect to the appraisal of any property, will the appraiser say to you, "Do you want a high value or a low value?" And here is where I want to say to the appraiser, "I want you to determine the fair value as it presently prevails, as you see the value." So it is that we are not quite that unique; we have a very special professional burden. And to fulfill that very special professional burden, I want us to understand what that burden is, and to effect essentially a 180 degree swing from the statements being predicated on the management bias to (and I am going to state it very bluntly) shift it from the management bias to the biases of the independent auditor with all his credentials underlined. Just as after the adversarial proceedings in the courts have gone their way, and the plaintiff's and defendant's adversaries have indicated their positions from their positions of bias, the ultimate judgment is then shifted to what? It is shifted to the biases of either the jury or the judge. And we are then ultimately left to the biases of the unbiased historian to write the history of that particular era.

IV.

Accounting and Realism

BY STANLEY SPORKIN

Previously Enforcement Director,
Securities and Exchange Commission

The accounting profession has proven its resiliency in the past decade. It has overcome some very troubling and trying times and is probably as strong and influential today as it has ever been. This is partly due to the deregulation movement presently impacting on every aspect of our business and professional lives. An integral part of this trend is to place more responsibility and reliance on the private sector.

I would submit that I do not believe the individual accounting firms or the public at large will be serving the best interests of the profession by not requiring the highest levels of performance. The accounting profession has much to offer our society. It is pivotal to the proper functioning of our economic system of capital formation. Without the accountant's opinion, the vast sums of money needed to fuel our system could not be raised. For the system to flourish we must insist the accounting profession be staffed with accountants that are both capable and possess the highest degree of integrity.

Over the years, the key concept that was the touchstone of the profession boiled down to essentially one word, namely, "independence." I do not doubt for one moment the extreme importance of that concept. Nor, may I add, that in many of the instances in which I witnessed a failed audit there existed a breach of this concept in its broadest application. Today, I would like to introduce a slightly different variation of the independence doctrine, and that is the concept of "realism."

I submit that many of the problem firms we are all familiar with, the financial statements and the accounting reports on them, reflected a lack of realism. How else can we explain the lack of any real warning with respect to the recent Penn Square Debacle? As late as March 1982, according to a recent newspaper report, the firm's accountant gave the firm, and I quote from the article, "A virtual clean bill of health." A member of the accounting firm is quoted as saying, "A financial statement by itself does not tell potential investors enough about the health of a company . . . It is nothing more than a snapshot of the bank's position on December 31, 1981." The article goes on to state: "What investors did not know is that Penn Square had been under special supervisory attention by the controller's office since early 1980, and that the public accounting firm had done a second analysis for management and directors that only highlighted weaknesses in the bank's policies and procedures."

In this case, as I understand it, there was a qualified report the year before with the typical discharge of the accounting firm bold enough to render that report. As I will mention later on, I believe something has to be done to discourage the taking of punitive action when an accounting firm, in upholding its independence and integrity, makes an unpopular call. I vividly remember chatting with the senior member of an accounting firm reviewing a blown audit. He was quite candid in his remarks. He said, "Mr. Sporkin, this case is an example of blind adherence to generally accepted accounting principles." In each of some ten different decisions, the accounting conventions permitted the treatment presented in the financial statements. What was lacking according to the senior accountant was that no one stepped back to review the statement as a whole and ask the very important question of whether the statement realistically presented the true financial position of the company. In this context, the whole may indeed be greater than its individual parts.

I found a very interesting phenomenon during my days at the SEC arising out of the merger and acquisition craze. It was normal practice for major firms considering the acquisition of other companies to have their accountants examine the target concerns, their books and records and provide the acquiring company with a true appraisal of what it was getting. I had occasion to review some of those reports and to compare them with the filed report that had been passed on by the company's own auditors. Too often the reports differed to such an extent that it was difficult to realize both referred to the same company.

The accounting literature is now replete with cases where the independent auditors simply ignored facts which they knew or were readily available to them. Let me just tick off some of the cases which should have become household names to the profession. In San Diego alone, we had the U.S. Financial and Westgage Financial Breakdowns. In both of these cases, there were serious questions concerning the treatment of transactions of related parties. Giant Stores, Inc., National Student Marketing, and Sterling Homex are the three additional examples of accounting failures that are "must reading" for all students of the profession. I can remember instances where accountants ignored stated Commission positions and, when later called to task on the matter, simply said they did not put much credence in the Commission's position. Indeed, in one particular case, the accountant performing the audit did not even think it was important enough to bring to the attention of his superiors at the firm the fact that the Commission had taken issue with the accounting treatment.

I have witnessed a number of instances where accountants in the conduct of their audits ignored the fact that the Commission had a current investigation of their client. In some instances the accountants did not even take time to delve into the matters under SEC investigation. In one case that I vividly remember, an accountant ignored an article that placed in question the business practices and integrity of a key person of a complex of companies that he was auditing. The article was actually found in the accountant's audit file and, when questioned as to what he did about it, the accountant replied that he did not believe it was relevant.

What I always found of interest was the position taken by many accountants that blind compliance with accounting standards or principles would immunize the accountant from any responsibility with respect to the accounting opinions rendered. Here we have placed in strongest focus the issue of whether accountants can ignore reality.

The point I am making was recently most graphically illustrated in a decision by the Ninth Circuit Court of Appeals, entitled SEC v. Seaboard Corporation, et. al. For those of you who are interested, the case was decided on May 24, 1982, and can be found in CCH Federal Securities Law Reports, Page 93, 618. I should caution you in reading the case that, although the decision was recently rendered, the underlying facts actually took place in the early 1970s. The case came before the appellate court for the most part on a procedural issue, namely, whether there were sufficient factual disputes to require a full trial of the case. The lower court had decided the case and awarded summary judgment in favor of the accounting firm.

Since the case was decided on a procedural issue, the court, for the purpose of its decision, in large part considered the allegations of the plaintiffs and affidavits from both officials of the plaintiff and the defendant, but without attempting to resolve the factual differences presented by those affidavits. At issue was a registration statement and prospectus of a company which it was alleged contained certain misrepresentations and omissions, as follows: (1) the company failed to disclose that it was having financial difficulty; (2) the company overstated its net worth by at least $500,000; (3) the company failed to disclose anticipated losses on incompleted projects; (4) the company stated it had some $12 million in back orders when in reality the true figures were much less; and (5) the company failed to disclose that the primary backlog customer was in fact controlled by it and was unable to pay for its back orders. It was also alleged that the audit cutoff date was chosen to cover up a recent period of poor earnings.

The accounting firm in its defense alleged that it had complied with generally accepted accounting principles. In an affidavit submitted by the auditor in charge of the audit, it was explained that the backlog was not audited because, "A backlog is not susceptible to audit because there is no way to verify supporting financial data." In support of his position, the auditor attached a copy of AICPA accounting standards that specifically directed accountants not to comment on backlogs. Regarding the extent of the auditor's participation in the preparation of the company's prospectus, the accountant in charge of the audit stated that he did not attend with the due diligence meetings with the underwriters and that he reviewed the registration documents only for the purpose of ensuring, "That no fact was being reported contrary to those in the financial statements."

The plaintiffs in the action submitted an affidavit for the purpose of showing that the accounting firm's involvement went beyond a mere audit of the financial statements and that it, in fact, knew of material misrepresentations and omissions in the prospectus and registration statement. The plaintiff's affidavit stated the accounting firm had the responsibility for preparing all the financial information to be included in the prospectus, that the accounting firm chose the cutoff date for the audit even though it knew that the company's financial condition deteriorated rapidly thereafter, and that the accounting firm's awareness of the financial deterioration of the company was supported by its possession of a balance sheet that was dated 30 days after the cutoff date. Furthermore, the affidavit showed that the accounting firm had long served as the company's auditors and had been involved with the company since its inception and that the company's management relied upon the auditing firm's expertise and made available all the financial information requested. The accounting firm regularly conversed and corresponded with the company about the prospectus, the accountant in charge of the audit read and commented on the full text of all drafts of the company's prospectus and registration statement, and just 9 days after the effective date of the offering, the accounting firm reported that a company that was affiliated with the issuer and was the customer generating a substantial part of the backlog, was a company without substance and was in fact organized by the issuer's personnel.

The court's language in overruling the District Court's grant of summary judgment is quite instructive. I quote:

> On this record, there appear to be material issues regarding (the accountant's) knowledge of and participation in the alleged misrepresentation. It asserts that summary judgment is proper because it must succeed as a matter of law with its defense of compliance with generally accepted accounting standards. We disagree. First, it is not clear on this record whether compliance with generally accepted accounting standards implies that (the accountant) did not know of the misrepresentation and omission that occurred. Nor is it clear that the accounting standard presented supports nonaudit of the backlog.
>
> Rather, viewing the document in the light most favorable to (the plaintiff), the standard applies only to audits relating to 'comfort letters' written pursuant to underwriting contracts and not to audits generally.
>
> Had (the accountant) asserted by affidavit facts indicating its ignorance of the misrepresentations being made, it may have met its burden. Because it has not made clear the state of its knowledge nor the implications of compliance with generally accepted accounting standards, we believe it has not.

In reading the opinion, I direct your attention to that part of footnote 15, which states:

> We assume that generally accepted accounting standards do not provide protection from liability when the accountant fails to reveal material facts which he knows or which, but for a deliberate refusal to become informed, he should have known should be revealed.

This is the second court that has rejected blind adherence to so-called generally accepted accounting standards as the basis for absolving accountants from any legal liability. The other case was the decision in U.S. v. Simon which can be found at 425 Federal Reporter 2nd, 796. Thus, in my view, an accountant cannot say that his presentation was based on generally accepted accounting principles or standards when he in fact knows that the presentation is a misleading one. In effect, the accountant cannot ignore reality.

I realize that some might accuse me of being naive and perhaps unrealistic in ignoring the fact that perhaps some accountants may ignore realism because it is not in their or their client's economic interest to tell it like it is. I accept that criticism, but I do have faith in the system. There have been untold numbers of cases in which the accountants have done the right thing. These, of course, are not set forth in the accounting literature. We have not yet learned of a way to report on cases that show the right way to do things.

I believe that our instruction on accounting matters can be vastly improved. I believe that there should and must be more classroom analysis of those matters that represent the so-called "blown audits" as well as examples of where the accounting work has been first class. I believe that we have all become much too technical in our teaching and application of accounting conventions and spend too much of our effort in attempting to develop what I call "cookbook accounting. "I think that we all seem to be more interested in training our young accountants "how to" instead of recognizing that it is also important, at least in some instances, to be instructive as to "how not to."

I also believe, as I mentioned before, that there need to be incentives for accountants that do the job the way they are supposed to. I have for some time recommended that a system of reparations be enacted to compensate the accounting firm that is discharged or otherwise disadvantaged for properly discharging its responsibilities in a manner its client has found unacceptable. Perhaps one or two years' audit fees should be the amount of reparations where there has been involuntary dismissal of the accounting firm.

Since I have an audience of academicians, I would like to leave you with some simple suggestions which I believe should be given some consideration in the training of our future auditors. Here are my suggested rules:

Rules of Realism in Accounting

1. Before an audit is commenced, the accountant should familiarize himself or herself completely with the company and its management. The accountant must also be aware of the industry in which the client is operating to determine the kind of business customs and business environment that prevail. Thus, when you are performing an audit in the gambling industry, you might want to bring a different kind of skepticism than with respect to some other industry. The accounting firm, as part of its preliminary work, should very carefully examine all transactions with persons closely affiliated with management, not only on a disclosed but also on an undisclosed basis if such relationships exist.

2. In all instances, an accountant should maintain a healthy skepticism.

3. The accountant should never lose sight of the audit as a whole.

4. Quality should be maintained as the highest priority in the audit.

5. An accountant should maintain a working knowledge of SEC and fraud literature.

6. It is important to be current on trends in corporate "gimmickry."

7. Decisions concerning the scope of the audit and

further testing should be based on all available information, including evaluations of management integrity and competency.

8. Where competitive principles are involved, the accountant should select the one that most realistically applies to the facts at hand.

9. Provide for close supervision of all audit work, and channels to easily move problems "up the line."

10. Reserve the right to make your own decisions. In other words, do not take your exception list into meetings with management and start to bargain away the items on the list. I remember one auditor who was very proud in having won four or five of the exceptions he made to the audit. Eighty percent is not a passing grade in this business.

11. At the completion of an audit, step back and ask yourself whether the financial statements truly reflect reality.

In my research for my presentation here today, I came across the following quotation that was contained in a paper prepared by Touche Ross & Company in 1975. I would like to leave you with that message:

> The goals of accounting are to measure, record, and communicate economic reality. In the long run, these goals are necessities--both for accounting and for society. Can behavior be economically rational if not grounded on economic reality?

I would remove the word "economic."

Discussion

OF

ACCOUNTING AND REALISM

PARTICIPANTS IN THE DISCUSSION

OF

STANLEY SPORKIN'S

PAPER

Mark Asman, Bowling Green State University

Wayne Bremser, Villanova University

Abraham Briloff, Baruch College, City University of New York

Barbara Merino, North Texas State University

Maurice Moonitz, University of California at Berkeley

Marilyn Neimark, Baruch College, City University of New York

Charles Tritschler, Purdue University

Discussion is introduced by Mr. Sporkin:

STANLEY SPORKIN:

Do we have any special responsibility for public interest? At the SEC, by charter, we only had the one interest, which was namely the interest of investors. But, when you really look to the interest of investors, I would dare say there are very few other constituents that would not be similarly protected. Even the company and its directors are protected if they abide by the rules, because they will not be sued or thrown into jail. And so, therefore, I always took that position even though we got into a number of different areas. For example, we got into the environment. That was not because I liked the environment - but when we brought a case against U.S. Steel, it was because there was inadequate disclosure concerning environmental problems. The same applied to Applied Chemical and also Occidental Petroleum. It had nothing to do with the public interest not being served; it was because there was a financial impact, and because a company that had involved itself in the environment was not disclosing what it was supposed to disclosure. Similarly, in the bribery cases: it was not a question that I did not like bribery; it was a question of certain of our public companies involving themselves in bribery and not disclosing it.

In these cases, the SEC played a consistent role. Now

there may be some instances where there was inconsistency. I do not know of any. But I do think there is a tremendous amount of consistency with the role of the SEC and that certain disclosures have to be made.

QUESTIONER:

In respect to your story, I was at a college class reunion about five or six years ago and one gentleman I went to school with was a divisional controller working in a multinational corporation. He talked about being on the bribery list, and the company won a substantial contract. He told of the incredible way the auditor sacrificed standards. This person's classmate, who was a partner for an investigating accounting firm, was apparently trying to get the audit, maybe not this year but maybe five years from now. Anyway, after more drinks, he repeated the story directly to the partner. The partner said, "Yeah, its really a tough game out there," and was not at all upset about sacrificing standards.

STANLEY SPORKIN:

It is interesting, but where does Abe Briloff and myself and others come from on this? We come out of our environment. And I must tell you, that you have no idea of the impact that you folks have on students, I believe that a lot can be done in the classroom. If those kids know from the very first day that compromising is not the standard, they are going to take that with them when they go into the profession. You would be surprised but it will work. I do not want you to think I am patting myself on the back, but at a time when I was in the midst of doing all these things, we at the SEC were the sole force that was really pushing the accounting profession. In all those years, I received five speaking requests. One was from Abe at Baruch, two were from my Alma Mater, Penn State, where I learned accounting. One was from the University of Maryland, because my kid goes to school there, and one from Princeton because they gave me an award. But that is it. What would it take to bring somebody to a school? We are not like Al Haig who charges $20,000 to be heard: You pay the expenses and that is it. But it seems to me it would be an enormously important thing for your students to be shown people who have done it; who have found out what has to be done; and what the cases are all about that connect these experiences with a course of studies. The course--you can call it the blown audit course, or the failed audit, or something like that--would cut across a broad section of studies and would help students deal with accounting principles. This would be a tremendous review for the students before they go out and take a CPA or go on further.

QUESTIONER:

Regarding one of the solutions that you came up with in

terms of the independence of the auditors it struck me that perhaps there is another way around it. Basically, if you are an auditor who satisfies management, you can be an auditor for life, the way the present situation is. It seems to me that we would certainly not tolerate this from the American presidency. Franklin Roosevelt thought about an amendment as a result of it. Also in Britain, universities are audited. You have an external examiner system, for example, in which all final exams are audited by a professor from another university. But this is for a fixed term. What I would like to suggest to you and perhaps you would comment on the fact, that maybe auditing firms should be for a fixed term: one, three, five years . . . ten years . . . whatever? Something along these lines so that the vested interests of the firm would not be to maintain the contract.

STANLEY SPORKIN:

It is now the case in most companies that they hire the auditor as part of the proxy each year. That is not the issue. We were toying with the idea when the question of rotating auditors came up of requiring new auditors every three years. That does not really work because the costs that are involved are tremendous. There is a tremendous start-up cost for a new firm coming in. I do not know what the answer is. To be fair, by and large, our accounting system is a unique system that we have, and it works. What we are focusing on are the exceptions; but the exceptions are hopefully a very small part of the system. I do think that there are several things that we have to do. One is the training aspect of it; that is, where you come in. You are probably saying, "This guy does not know what he is talking about, that he has not been in a classroom in thirty years." But if I am right, then this is one place to start. We will make a course that has some relevance to this world--instead of debits and credits, instead of having a bookkeeping course. Second, we must have proper insight. The one thing that I prided myself on was the fact that we were a radar screen. And as long as the accountants knew that they could be picked up for speeding, now and then, there was incentive to do what was right. Because the last thing an accountant wants to do is lose his ticket, because if he loses his ticket, he loses his income. So, therefore, you do need effective oversight and proper training. The third thing I did at the SEC was to determine who goes on that bus. In every case where you have a financial failure, we have to examine the failure and do as a pathologist does: To find out what was the cause of the failure and who participated in it. Accountants have a very important role to perform, and part of the system is to have them there so that you do not have surprises. You are always going to have failures, but what the system cannot tolerate is surprises. In other words, you are told that a company is in bad shape, then nobody is going to be unexpectedly hurt—nobody is going to feel like they have been taken in. But accountants have to assure us that there are not going to be surprises or jolts in the system. Thus, we have to determine what their role is. I think that if you have vigorous and strong oversight, with the proper training, you could have a pretty good system—with reparation provisions at the end. If the accounting firm does what it is supposed to do, and gets thrown out, they ought to get their audit fees for a certain period of time. Now you might say, "How can that be done? We need another rule." No, you do not need another rule. You can probably do it in one of several ways. One by contract: If the auditor is providing fine services, and he is discharged because he issued a qualified opinion, then the SEC ought to have a mechanism to determine whether it is a bona fide discharge and if not, to ensure that the accountant is not economically disadvantaged for doing his job. For example, there could be an arbitration panel where both the company and the accounting firm could each select somebody, and then the two would select the third. If that all was determined, then they would get two years' fees for doing nothing! Now why did I say that? It is because of the dislocation and the real loss to that accounting firm's business, that they should have the money for a period of time. Two years is a good enough period for a firm to be able to go out and get another client or clients to build up that loss of revenue. So it can be done even without regulation if the accountants are willing to do it.

It could be ordered by a self-regulatory organization, for example, the New York Stock Exchange. They could say that all firms listed with them must have in their contract a reparations clause. We did a lot with the New York Stock Exchange; the audit committee was done with the New York Stock Exchange. We said it was too much to ask that every company has to have an independent audit committee because there are some little companies that could not meet these standards. So we said, "Let us just take the blue chip companies, those that belong to the New York Stock Exchange." They looked at it and said, "It sounds like a good rule," and they put it in. That is why you have independent audit committees. That is the way this thing could work and, if you had that kind of thing in place, I you would see a pretty good system.

QUESTIONER:

One of your themes you keep going back to is "reality" or "realistic," but you did not define it. I do not know what you are saying. Do you mean economic reality, professional reality, social reality—your reality might be like Star Wars?

STANLEY SPORKIN:

I have always found that realism is one of the best

words that probably exists in the dictionary. I remember applying it in many other ways. For example, when we were talking about dealing with which companies should be exempted from certain regulations, I came up with, "It has to be a real company." It is a real company if it has operations. Does it have a product that it sells? Does it have revenues? We were able to use that kind of thing to start out with, because there are plenty of companies that are not real, they are shells. They are set up for a particular circumstances, and you do not want to give them certain benefits.

What I am talking about in accounting and realism is that you do not sit down and say: "These are the rules that I learned in college or graduate school," and start applying them blindly. What are the facts? How realistic is it when we apply that statement? For example, if you know you are auditing in an industry such as the gambling industry, where you know that a prevalence of skimming takes place, is it realistic to start applying standards without taking into account the realities of the company and industry? What would you take into account? You would make sure that there were sufficient tests that were made, or that there was a system that was adopted by the company to ensure that there was no skimming or just a minimum of skimming. That is what I mean by realism. You know you are dealing with a real company in an industry that is fraught with all kinds of problems.

What, therefore, can you do to make sure that when your work comes out at the end, it is a realistic appraisal of that company and what that company stands for. What I am saying is that we need an awareness and understanding of what goes on around you. I saw the things that got screwed up. When we go into a gambling company, and there were millions of dollars of skimming taking place, the person said, "I did not realize Mr. X ran that company, and he was a person that we had to watch. We did not realize who X was." There are many ways of defining it. It is what is known as "street-smarts." When you are in the street, what do you have to know? What do you have to look out for? What do you have to worry about? It is that kind of concept. Sorry, I cannot give you a dictionary definition.

QUESTIONER:

What you are talking about here is integrity; and we do not teach integrity. Integrity is something that does not apply just to accounting, it applies to every profession: Medicine, law, accounting. You are talking about integrity, you are talking about substance over form. This is not something you teach; you can attempt to and set it as an ideal, but you do not teach students this. Students learn this by emulating others. Certainly we should attempt to teach it but it is not something easily taught. And the other thing that I do not agree with is that we pay the accountant two years' reparations for doing that which he should be doing anyway. So what you are talking about—I hold that you are a 100 percent correct—this is what we should attempt to be doing in the classroom. You cannot tell a student or an individual how they will or will not behave. When the decision comes, or it is presented to the individual that they must behave with integrity, then all the forces on that individual at that particular point in time will be the deciding factor.

STANLEY SPORKIN:

I am trying to avoid using the word integrity because I think you can be realistic without necessarily mixing that concept up with integrity.

QUESTIONER:

I do not, that is a compromise.

STANLEY SPORKIN:

I was using realism as a concept that assumed integrity existed. But let us assume that a person is found out because he used what I call my "realistic test." And he says, "Okay, I am realistic, and I know that this company is doing all these bad things." Now, he then might decide that, for one reason or another, he is going to ignore it. That is one set of priorities.

QUESTIONER:

That is wrong, that is the absence of integrity.

STANLEY SPORKIN:

I am sorry, I do not say that what I am suggesting here was right.

QUESTIONER:

I know, I realize you are not. I am suggesting that what you are talking about is a human behavioral factor that does not necessarily apply to accounting.

STANLEY SPORKIN:

Hopefully, he comes out with the right answer. What I am asking is that teachers help him get to the right answer. Later on, the law authorities will have to deal with him if he wants to become a totally dishonest person. But remember, there have been very few cases that I have seen where you have the accountant facing up to the fact that he made a dishonest decision. First of all, it is very hard to prove and secondly, I think that in many of the instances, the accountant never got to the point where he can say, "I am lacking integrity." When he gets to that point he can say, "I can rationalize what I am doing," (as Abe mentioned) "because there is something in the literature that says that this is appropriate to be done."

QUESTIONER:

Then he is not acting professionally.

STANLEY SPORKIN:

If we had teachers who said, "Okay, come out with the right decision," I would be extraordinarily happy. And even happier if he has integrity. I agree with that. But I assume that basic concept.

But try to put yourself in a position of how do you get people to get to the point where they have all the facts to make the decision. I have found, in too many instances, accountants being so narrow that they never even have the data or the information from which they can make the decision to be dishonest.

QUESTIONER:

But it is because there is a penalty for an adverse decision in society. That is what makes "acting professionally" so difficult.

STANLEY SPORKIN:

The first point that I wanted to make is the one you took me up on: Reparations for the accountant who is only doing his job. An accounting firm ought not to be penalized for doing the job.

QUESTIONER:

But they should not be rewarded for doing what they ought to be doing.

STANLEY SPORKIN:

I do not want to reward them, I do not want to penalize them, and they get penalized when they get fired. Look, if I were going to go out and work for somebody, I would always want a severance provision in the contract. Not that you need a contract for 5 years, or 10 years. But when those five years come up, you ask, "Am I going to be rehired?" The critical thing that you want in any contract or an appointment, is what I call severance provision. What is a severance provision? A severance provision says that they have a year or two years of cushion to be able to do what they have to do. Why? Because without it you lose your independence.

QUESTIONER:

I understand you.

STANLEY SPORKIN:

The accountants are entitled to have that. Nobody is being hurt by that; the company is not being hurt.

QUESTIONER:

We are still rewarding people for doing what they are

paid to do. That is the danger of this profession, the medical profession--any profession where that person must have integrity.

STANLEY SPORKIN:

I am not rewarding them, I am saying that nothing prevents two people from sitting down and agreeing over a severance provision. I am giving them an idea of how they can implement this at the beginning of a relationship and not when there is a problem at the end. So that, therefore, they are really being paid for what they are doing.

QUESTIONER:

You started out saying that accountants are not concerned with the public interest, or that is not their job. The second thing you said was that the SEC mandate was to investors. The first question, Nader's criticisms of the FCC and other consumer criticisms, have said that its mandate is to investors, not public interest, and Nader contends that the two are not necessarily congruent. The second point I would like you to give a response to is, if auditing or if accounting does not focus on the public interest, and if one assumes that we live in an oligopolistic society, what do we have to protect the public interest?

STANLEY SPORKIN:

I do not want to sound so cavalier with respect to the public interest, but I hope that I have demonstrated that there is no inconsistency between what a statute tells you to do, and the public interest. The problem that I have is that we have not even arrived at first base. You know, I have always looked at myself as a pragmatic person, not satisfied with talking in pompous terms and then getting nothing accomplished. But in trying to take those small steps, you will see something happening. If you look at me objectively, what one person can do in a system, you are going to be in awe. It is the kind of thing that Professor Lindblom mentioned previously about government working. I believe it did work, it was not just me, it was Pollack, and Levine, Summer, and Burton. If only we can get government working the way it is supposed to, or get a statute to function the way it is supposed to function. If you read the basic securities laws, they talk about protection of investors. And that is why anybody with my job has to be looking to protect the investor. I contend or submit to you that if I started to try to put my own views of what I thought the public interest was, we would have failed. There was a person who wrote a book about me telling how I did all these things that I was not supposed to do; it was nonsense. But if that occurs after doing what you are supposed to do, can you imagine what that book would have said if I did what I was not supposed to do?

There is still so much that has to be done within the mandate of the various provisions of the laws. That is where I would differ from Nader. You do not have to get to the "public interest" or the "public sector at large." If you just did what the statute says you are supposed to do, you would be surprised what end total you would find; yes, you may not get to 100%, but 80%, 70%, or even 60% is still good.

QUESTIONER:

I would like to find out what response you received to your two-year severance idea. And I will tell you why: Because I think there is a basic naivete in believing that the accountant is this great person of integrity coming down on the white horse. Academics have been accused that they have never had to sweat in front of a client. Now, when the client shows you the book, and the tenderfoot way he can record inventory, and starts talking about judgments as to what the allowance for doubtful accounts should be, and what should be the position for obsolete inventory, you do have problems and could conceivably lose a client. Now it seems to me that it is awfully late to talk about independence when that guy on the other end of the table is paying your fee. But at least I think that, if I have the two years of severance, while I may not have as much backbone as I would like to have, I will have a little more than the system currently allows me to have. But what was the reaction?

STANLEY SPORKIN:

I said it several times, and no one picked it up. I will leave it up to you, I am out of that business now but I do think it can work. You do not need a rule, you do not need a law. Look, when somebody wants you prior to an engagement, and they think that you are the only person in the world, they are not anticipating that you are going to walk from the audit in two years. You start with two, maybe you will cut down to one; but at least you have got something. But it can be done contractually.

QUESTIONER:

Do you ever have to answer questions like this (do not answer if you have not before): The efficient market will protect investors; we do not need the SEC?

STANLEY SPORKIN:

I forgot one college that I was invited to in Chicago that I did speak at! Some of the people there did not want to even regulate medicine, and they were going to permit my mother-in-law's chicken soup to be used to cure cancer. It was that kind of a thing that the efficient market will work. My view is that if you take something to the "nth degree," it is an absurdity. Just as if you go the other way: That we can cure all ills if we have a society run just by our government. Obviously that is wrong. You need government, it has an important role to play. Most important in helping the individual gain the bargaining power so that the individual can gain the rewards and the benefits of society that we want them to have. The government can ensure the equality of treatment out there, more than anything else. And if it does this, then it has gone a long way.

QUESTIONER:

What about extending your ideas of severance pay internally, within the staff of a major firm. When I went into accounting with one of the Big Eight, I was a little older than almost everybody; I was probably the oldest guy on staff. Early on in the job, there was a situation that arose that I thought we knew absolutely nothing about. What about the idea of having an insurance program that would be paid for by the CPA profession?

STANLEY SPORKIN:

That sounds like a good idea, like a workmen's compensation or an unemployment kind of thing. I think it is a good idea; the only problem is that I do not think that the profession would be able to philosophically accept it.

QUESTIONER:

With that line of thinking, I find it difficult to believe that clients would go for the reparations idea. All the CPA firms will have to demand the same type of thing, or it is likely that the client would just go to another firm.

STANLEY SPORKIN:

Yes, that is why I recommend that it be done at the beginning of the relationship. Your point is that you will need some legislation. And if the accounting firms try to do it amongst themselves, I think they will have an antitrust problem. So I think you will need some kind of sanction. My problem is that under the mood we are living in now, it is very difficult to get any legislation.

QUESTIONER:

Getting back to the idea of ignorance versus the lack of integrity. How much of the problem is due to ignorance versus lack of integrity?

STANLEY SPORKIN:

As I said before, I found very few demonstrated cases where you have the "crooked" accountant. And the profession itself can take pride in that fact. There are very few cases where you will find the accountants on the take. Would you agree with that, Abe?

ABRAHAM BRILOFF:

Mr. Nixon said, "I am no crook," and the profession similarly would say that. However, the question is, what does integrity mean? If it means that somehow you could find something in the NARS system—if you look hard enough, where you could find a precedent in there and say, "Now we can show the discount on this income." I would say it is a lack of integrity. But if you asked Touche Ross they would say, "No, we followed the rules." They are not crooks. But they lack integrity as I would define integrity but not as Touche Ross did.

QUESTIONER:

I was surprised because you seem to be indicating that there was a real ignorance in many cases. I guess I was under the impression that was sort of an excuse, people were using ignorance as an excuse in court so that they do not get nailed. But in the final analysis, what it really revealed was a lack of integrity. The whole first part of your speech—maybe you had some part in writing it—but Peat, Marwick, and Mitchell, when they bring in a new audit person, the first thing they do is take him into a room for about forty-five hours and give him the same speech that you gave us today.

STANLEY SPORKIN:

They did not write my speech.

QUESTIONER:

I know, maybe you helped them write it, but they show you a film on the accountant's legal liability. They go through all the cases. They tell you all those very same points. Look at the big picture. Do not get caught in this; do not what they did over here. I feel that somehow, if you want to learn how to be a good accountant, you can. It is available through the Big Eight firms or through your own personal endeavor. Maybe I am afraid that some people do not want to learn.

STANLEY SPORKIN:

The accountant does not know how to handle certain circumstances. For example, he does not know what it means when he reads a newspaper article about somebody, and how to figure it into his audit. You would be surprised! Where I am now, I am the oldest person there. But I see some young lawyers coming in that are terribly naive in dealing with real life situations. We use the term "judgment;" there is something called "an intuitive sense" that is involved in many things, and you would be surprised how few young people have that intuitive sense and are able to say, "No, there is something wrong here." What I call, "the hard-core," instead of the "soft-core" cases. I only found one or two instances where an accountant was taking money under the table. Indeed, I found it more with lawyers than accountants. And the opportunities are there. If you are going to do something that is wrong, do it for the big bucks, do not do it for the change, it does not make any sense. Abe points out somebody shaving a point and he tries to, in effect, find some basis for doing what he is doing. I think there is some of that but it is a very difficult kind of thing to prove. He had it in one case where he could prove it. But if we can at least sensitize our people into realizing "what are the red flags" and how to cope with those red flags, I think that would be an important step.

V.

Accounting for Unequal Exchange Wealth Accumulation Versus Wealth Appropriation

BY TONY TINKER

New York University and
Baruch College, City University of New York

INTRODUCTION

Reviews that merely summarize the views of others are hardly worth writing. A successful review transcends the original and contributes on its own merits by putting the original "in its place" in helping the reader see a larger vision of things.

Professors Briloff, Lindblom, and Mr. Sporkin, in their very different ways, offer us important criticisms of contemporary accounting practices and specific proposals for moving beyond those practices. What still remains to be done, however, is to sketch out a map of the overall terrain; one that enables us to see the interrelations between Lindblom's, Briloff's, and Sporkin's remarks, and how each set of proposals relates to existing accounting practice and (what we might consider to be) a vista of the "total" accounting problematic. Figure 1 shows these ideas schematically.

FIGURE 1

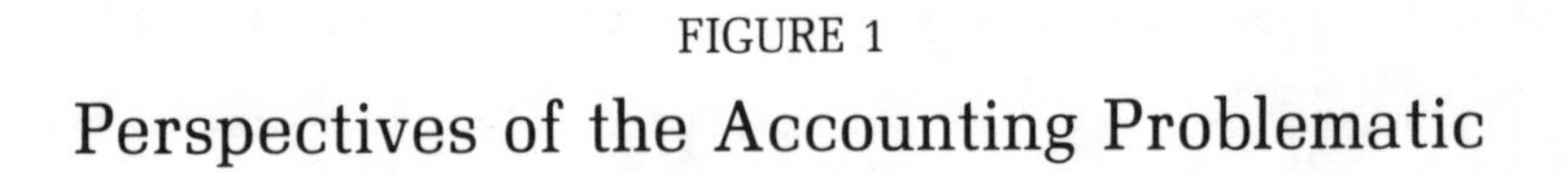

Perspectives of the Accounting Problematic

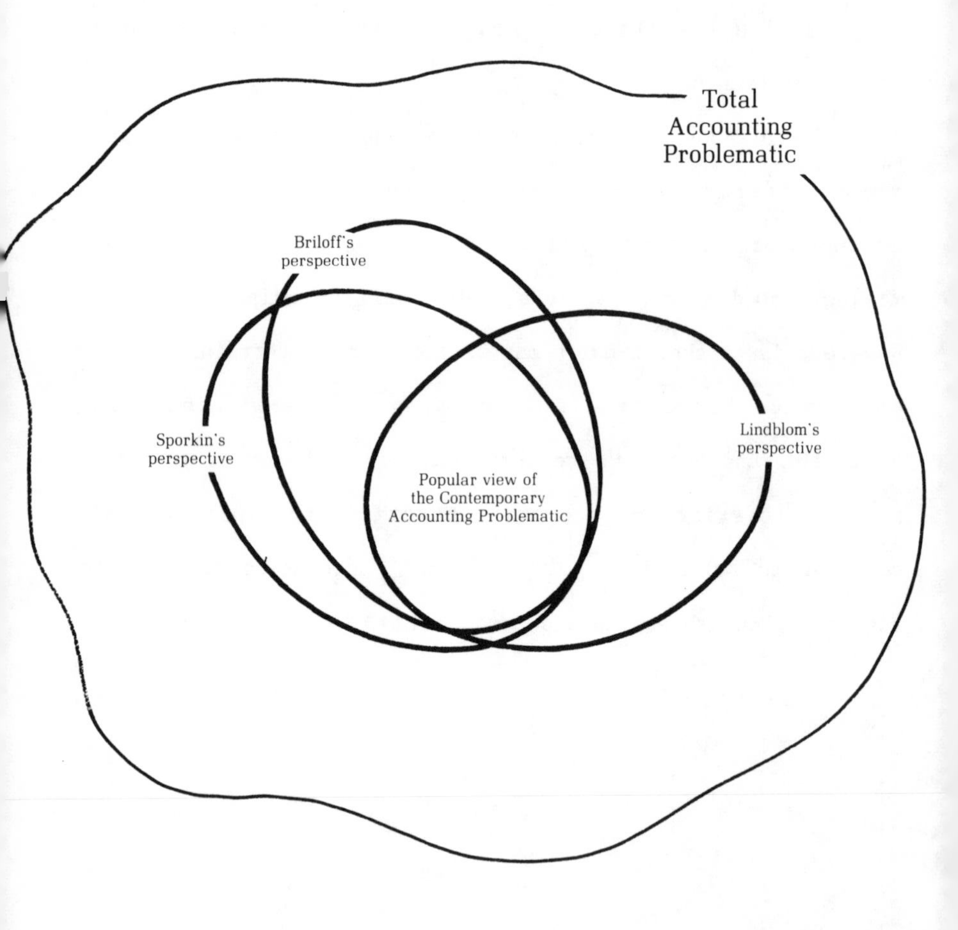

Figure 1 should not be taken too literally. It is intended to provide an impressionistic sketch of the aims of this review. A more precise formulation will be developed in subsequent passages. In Figure 1, the set entitled, "Contemporary Accounting Problematic" encompasses those problems and issues that are commonly regarded as part of the realm of accounting. (The broken line circumscribing this set reflects the inexact boundaries of contemporary practice). The perspectives of our three distinguished contributors are shown as both encompassing, and extending beyond, the Contemporary Accounting Problematic. The overlap between these three viewpoints represents their degrees of agreement; the uniqueness of each viewpoint is shown as their complements (the non-overlapping portions of the sets). Clarifying the commonalities and uniquenesses of each of these three perspectives is an important aim of this paper.

Finally, the figure suggests that the perspectives of our three contributors may fall short of disclosing the "total" accounting problematic. The key element in this review lies in developing a concept of the "total" accounting problematic that is based, not on orthodox notions of wealth, income, or profit, but on that of alienation. It will be argued in subsequent sections that alienation is a more fundamental category of social and individual welfare than economic wealth. Alienation belongs to older, classical systems of thinking that date back to the Greeks. Economic welfare is a more recent neo-classical mode of thought that deals only with a minority of the questions addressed by theories of alienation.

Insofar as accountants have explored the theoretical foundations of their subject, they invariably appeal to concepts of economic wealth and welfare, and virtually ignore notions of alienation. This review contends that, in different ways, our three contributions demonstrate the shortcomings of wealth-oriented notions of welfare, and the superiority of alienation-based perspectives. Here, a four-level hierarchy of alienation is explored; each level encompassing the levels below it and, in addition, incorporating new forms of alienation. Using this hierarchy, we can begin to enumerate an array of potential accounting systems, each differing from the others in terms of the variety of alienation each is capable of detecting. With such a theoretical formulation, it then becomes possible to classify our three contributors' accounting proposals according to the range of alienating behavior each would reveal.

CORPORATE PERFORMANCE: ALIENATION VERSUS WEALTH ACCUMULATION

The concept of alienation contrasts, in several significant ways, with that of "profit" and other wealth-related concepts that conventional accounting systems seek to measure and disclose (e.g. historical earnings, realizable profit, replacement cost profit, current value, present value). As an index of wealth accumulation, profit depicts human and social welfare as growth in the size of the "cake" available to a social collectivity. In this view, profit is the surplus or excess, after replenishing resources consumed (costs).

Despite the ubiquity of profit in the economic and accounting literature, it is a grossly inadequate metric of institutional performance. Typically, we are interested, not only in the total size of the cake, but also in how it is divided up or distributed. Interestingly, although the "academic" literature has been most reluctant to acknowledge distributional problems, the modern popular financial press is replete with criticisms of accountants arising out of scandals involving distributional issues. Today we find numerous examples of such controversies: Have managers made exorbitant salaries by consuming income that rightly belongs to the owners? Have insider traders abused their privileged positions as the stewards and custodians of the owner's assets by making unjustified gains? Is the corporate income tax expense overstated (thereby exaggerating the "cost of government" in the public's mind, and increasing pressure to reduce taxes and redistribute income away from the state to managers and shareholders)? Are employee pension expenses insufficient to meet pension obligations?

No amount of perfection of profit measurement will help resolve these kinds of questions; it is ironic, therefore, that the accounting literature has been almost exclusively concerned with the measurement of aggregate surplus (income and wealth measurement) and has virtually ignored distributional problems.

Below, we will explore the meaning of alienation and see that, not only are distributional issues inextricably tied to problems of alienation, but more important, all accounting problems are really problems of alienation.

ALIENATION IN SOCIAL THEORY

In this most general form, alienation refers to being "out of control." Humankind may be regarded as being "out of control" (alienated) in two specific ways. The first mode of alienation—anthropological alienation—is already familiar to economic-accounting research, but it exists under a different guise: it refers to man's struggle for existence against natural forces. Early periods of human development were characterized by a dependence on and subservience to natural rhythms and elements. Nature is out of man's control in the sense that economic progress and the development of human potentialities are restrained by man's ability to harness natural forces to his own advantage. Developments in productive techniques (the forces of production) represent accomplishments in reversing anthropological alienation.

It is in the above sense that contemporary economists and accountants are most acquainted with the term "alienation": As a state of economic underdevelopment that is remedied by a "more efficient utilization of economic resources" (neo-classical economics), or "by increasing social production through the division of labor" (classical economics). Petty, Smith, Mills, Betham,Hobbes, Hegel, Feuerbach, and many other early social philosophers, saw developments in productive capacity—through the social division of labor—as "the wealth of nations" and the primary means for overcoming anthropological alienation. It is in this first sense that accounting scholars are most familiar with the concept of alienation: As an anthropological condition of deprivation that is eradicated by technological progress and the accumulation of wealth. Indeed, some would argue that the primary social function of financial statements is to aid wealth (capital) accumulation, and thereby minimize anthropological alienation.

The genesis of anthropological alienation lies in man's economic struggle against nature. In contrast, social alienation originates in the struggle between man and man. This second form of alienation incorporates all forms of deprivation and estrangement that are "built-in" because of the very structure of the society in question. Masters and slaves, lords and serfs, and capitalists and workers, are broad classes of citizens that are distinguished by their differing rights, obligations, and entitlements to the means of subsistence. Inequalities in rights and entitlements are structural in that they are universal to all parts and members of the social system under examination. In fact, these social relations of class inequality are considered to be sufficiently important that they are used as a basis for defining social systems and distinguishing one system from another. Under slavery, for example, the ruling class owns natural resources, the tools of production, and members of the slave class; and these social relations may be distinguished from those found under certain forms of feudalism, where the vassal maintains economic possession of land and the tools of production as long as homage and service are paid to the lord. Each social system is defined by what is termed, the "social relations of production."

Alienated social relations are expressed in "unequal exchanges" between different social classes. Thus, a slave may spend six days producing commodities that are consumed by others, and receive, as recompense for sustenance, commodities the manufacture of which requires only one day's labor power.

Under the Labor Theory of Value, these relations of inequality take on a quantitative and objective form. Capitalism, for example, may be defined by the social relations existing between two classes; one that secures its means of subsistence through property ownership, the other through the sale of wage labor. The unequal relation between these two social classes is expressed—objectively and quantitatively—in the labor time embodied in the commodities that each provides in the sphere of exchange. Capitalists—qua capitalists—invest no labor in social production, even though they receive through exchange goods that contain the labor time of other social members. Laborers, in contrast, qua laborers, receive through exchange commodities embodying less labor time than the amount that they expend in production. This deficiency, in the aggregate, is equal to the total "surplus" (sic.) appropriated by capitalists. "Unequal exchange" refers precisely to this phenomenon, as the exchange, between social classes, of commodities containing unequal amounts of social labor. Ricardo first stumbled on this "inequality," referring to it as an "error" or "deviation;" but it was Marx who articulated the "error" into dynamic theory of social change.

Anthropological alienation and social alienation share a common core of meaning in that they both refer to the estrangement of man from his essence: Alienation implies obstacles and impediments—natural or social—that prevent man from realizing his/her full capacities and potentials. Thus, for Sartre and Heidegger, alienation is a state of forlorness of the human condition thereby stressing the subjective misery and deprivation that may ensue from objective inequality and disadvantage.

Alienation is not restricted to its social and anthropological forms; although there are persuasive arguments that would assign primary status to these forms. Sexual and racial oppression, for instance, are also forms of alienation that coexist with structural forms of domination. Whatever its forms however, alienation is an appropriation of the human essence, an impediment to human growth and development, and this is frequently reflected in an unequal exchange: an appropriation of labor time from one social constituency to another. In terms of the earlier parlance, alienation theory is not only interested in increasing the size of the social "cake," but also in raising distributional questions as to the manner in which the cake is divided up.

Here we encounter the first important connection with accounting. Accounting records transactions between different socioeconomic agents; alienation theory is concerned with exploitation through such relationships. Accountants are already familiar with a range of alienating transactions that have created a good deal of controversy within the profession: Appropriations from outside shareholders to "insiders" enabled by the latter's informational advantages; appropriations from employees through inadequate health and safety provisions, or through insufficient contributions to pension schemes;

appropriation of a local community's "free goods" (natural bounty) by polluting its environment; appropriations from women and racial minorities through discriminatory practices; appropriations from third world peoples, through commodity prices and wages held low by coercion and repression, etc.

These, and many other alienating transactions or "unequal exchanges," could appear on an income statement of an enterprise that is deemed quite profitable in conventional terms. What alienation theory suggests is that accounting not only needs a way of appraising "the bottom line," but rather "every line" to see whether the underlying transactions represent equal or exploitative exchanges in the sense described previously.

Figure 2 shows, in the form of a hierarchy, different levels of alienation and their relation to accounting. Anthropological alienation, reflecting man's struggle to overcome and harness nature to fulfill his needs, has an asocial and technical character that corresponds with the conventional accounting focus on profit and wealth accumulation. This form of alienation is described as Fiduciary Alienation in Figure 2. The higher levels in the hierarchy in Figure 2 encompasses social alienation. Thus, the concept of alienation aimed for here is one that is broad enough to subsume the conventional focus on profit, earnings, and surplus increments to wealth--growth in the size of the cake--and, at the same time, allows us

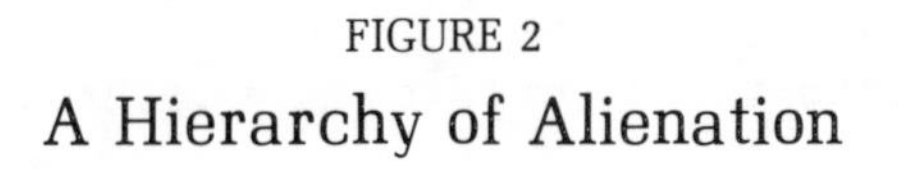

FIGURE 2

A Hierarchy of Alienation

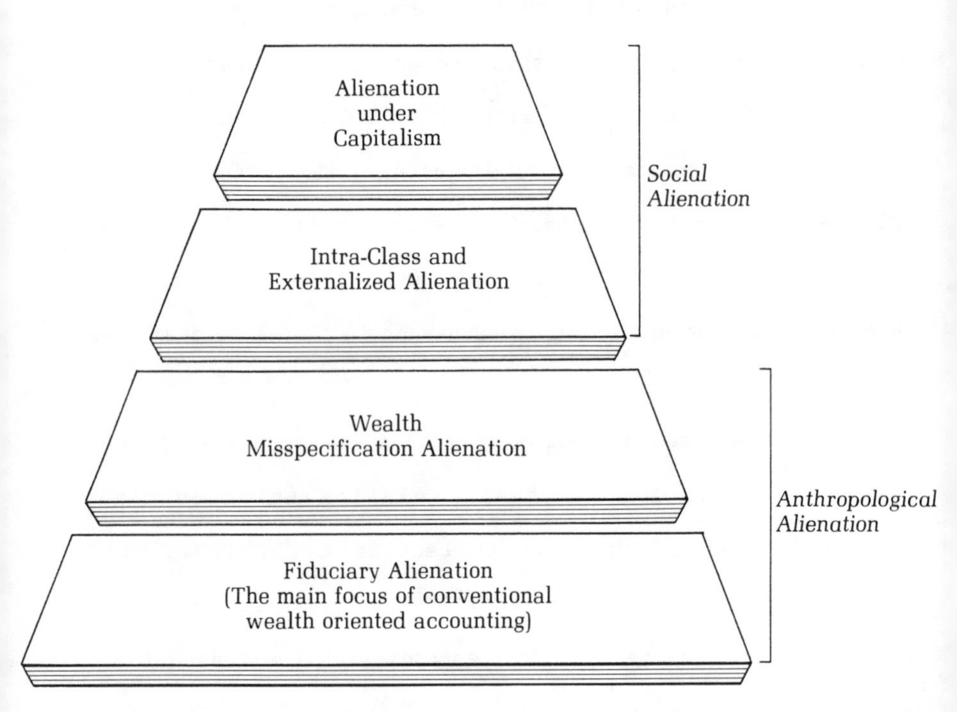

to examine degrees of conflict over income distribution--how the cake is divided.

LEVELS OF ALIENATION

In Figure 2, Fiduciary Alienation represents the owner's loss of control over the wealth that arises in large corporations as a result of the separation of ownership and control. Managers stand in a fiduciary relationship to the shareholders in that they are entrusted with the owner's assets. In addition, managers stand in a fiduciary relationship with trade creditors, banks, and other constituencies (some would argue society itself) all of whom have relinquished control over resources to management. Conventional accounting helps counterbalance this "loss of control"--Fiduciary Alienation--by reporting on management's conduct and assisting in monitoring management's behavior.

Wealth Misspecification Alienation, the second level in Figure 2, recognizes, as alienation, misspecifications in the corporation's "real" economic value. Such misspecifications are alienating in that, by misforming shareholders and other parties about the "real" value of the corporation, they can cause misallocations of resources and exacerbate the manager's task of controlling wealth accumulation. Wealth Misspecification Alienation is a misallocation of resources due to misinformation that causes wealth transfers at "incorrect" values. Only perfect foresight as to a corporation's future earnings could avert this type of alienation because only then would it be possible to discern the present, "real" economic value of corporate decisions. Ironically, this form of alienation has earned more attention in the accounting literature than any other form. It is included here because it is part (albeit a small part) of the total picture of alienation that accountants have struggled to deal with.

The next level of alienation shown in the figure incorporates two additional categories: Intra-Class Alienation and Externalized Alienation. Intra-Class Alienation arises because of the rivalry and competition that exists between factions within the stockholder group. Insider trading is an example. Here, one group of stockholders may expropriate the wealth of other stockholders if they exploit the information advantages conferred by their privileged position as insiders (e.g. managers, auditors, bankers). Conventional accounting ignores such appropriations because it insists on seeing a corporation exclusively as an entity thereby failing to observe the gains and losses between fractions of capital. Indeed, there is an explicit rule in conventional accounting that gains and losses (through a reissue of old shares, for instance) should not be recognized because a corporate entity cannot make a profit by trading with itself.

Externalized Alienation arises from the "side-effects" of corporate behavior that is not registered in the corporation's profitability calculations, but nevertheless materially affect the well-being of other institutions and members of the community. These side-effects are called externalities; they would be detected by an accounting system that took an overall, societal perspective; but they are ignored by conventional accounting systems that focus exclusively on the corporate entity.

The final level of alienation in the figure is that arising from capitalist relations of production. Capitalist alienation incorporates forms of alienation that only become apparent when we recognize the structural inequalities that define capitalism as a social system. From a sociological perspective, the defining characteristics of capitalism--as a social system--are the unique rights and entitlements over the means of subsistence (economic wealth and income) that are enjoyed by different social classes. In contrast with, say, feudal, slave or Asiatic society, capitalism protects property rights (restrictions on access to, use of, and consumption of property) and supports the property owner's claim to societal income without requiring any personal participation in the social production of that income. "Free" wage owners, in contrast, are not given any basic guarantees as to income or employment, but must sell their labor power in order to survive.

In a class perspective, property owners and laborers differ in one important respect: Their unequal opportunities for securing the means of subsistence. For capitalists, the property qualification is sufficient to provide income; no personal effort is needed. For labor, access to natural and other life-sustaining substances is barred; work is a precondition for obtaining income, and there is no assurance that work will always be forthcoming. These conditions are hardest on those at the periphery of the capitalist system; here, millions of people are denied opportunities to work and access to means of subsistence. Inequality in social rights between the laboring and the capitalist classes is a defining characteristic of capitalism. It is also the primary source of capitalist alienation in that one class—through the exercise of its rights—dominates and deprives other social members of life-sustaining substances and conditions.

When related to modern capitalism, the above view of social conflict might appear overly simplistic in that citizens are not just workers or just capitalists, but both. For many people, income is obtained, not just from working, but also from investments in pension plans, savings accounts, etc. Similarly, we rarely find a "pure" capitalist, rather capital owners often participate in the management of enterprises.

These complications do not invalidate the earlier

analysis of social conflict however, because the latter is not intended to assign individuals to one class or another. The analysis envisages that individuals assume a multiplicity of often contradictory roles that could create instability and conflict for role incumbent. For example, the analysis acknowledges that, as small investors and consumers, people may take advantage of benefits from cheap overseas production of goods and services, and in doing so help endanger their own position as employees. Such circumstances highlight the ambiguous role-set of the individuals under capitalism: citizens may contribute to their own alienation insofar as advantages secured in one realm may be attained at a cost to other realms.

If the relationship between alienation and accounting is discussed at all in the accounting literature, emphasis is given only to passive considerations where accounting merely "perceives" (reports) different degrees of alienation. But conventional accounting also plays a direct, proactive role in perpetuating alienation, through its omissions. By continuing to give a narrow and restricted picture of alienation, conventional accounting allows alienation to continue by default. The full extent and impact of this selective perception in conventional accounting is revealed when we contrast the focus of conventional accounting with its potential domain of interest in Figure 2. The difference between these two reflects the shortsightedness or ideological biases inherent in contemporary accounting.

ALTERNATIVE ACCOUNTING SYSTEMS

We extend Figure 2 in Figure 3 by juxtaposing "what accounting is" with "what accounting could be." With Figure 3, we can envisage a whole spectrum of accounting systems, differing only in terms of their capacities for recognizing various levels of social domination and alienation. These systems are ordered hierarchically in terms of their "perceptiveness," "consciousness" or "sensitivity" to alienation. The figure shows contemporary accounting at the lowest level of perceptiveness, and portrays the most enlightening, emancipatory form of accounting at the highest.

The hierarchies of alienation and accounting systems in Figure 3 provide the framework that can be used to analyze and classify the proposals of our contributors. It should be stressed that, apart from the Conventional Accounting, all the other accounting systems are hypothetical in that they still

FIGURE 3

Alienation and Accounting Consciousness

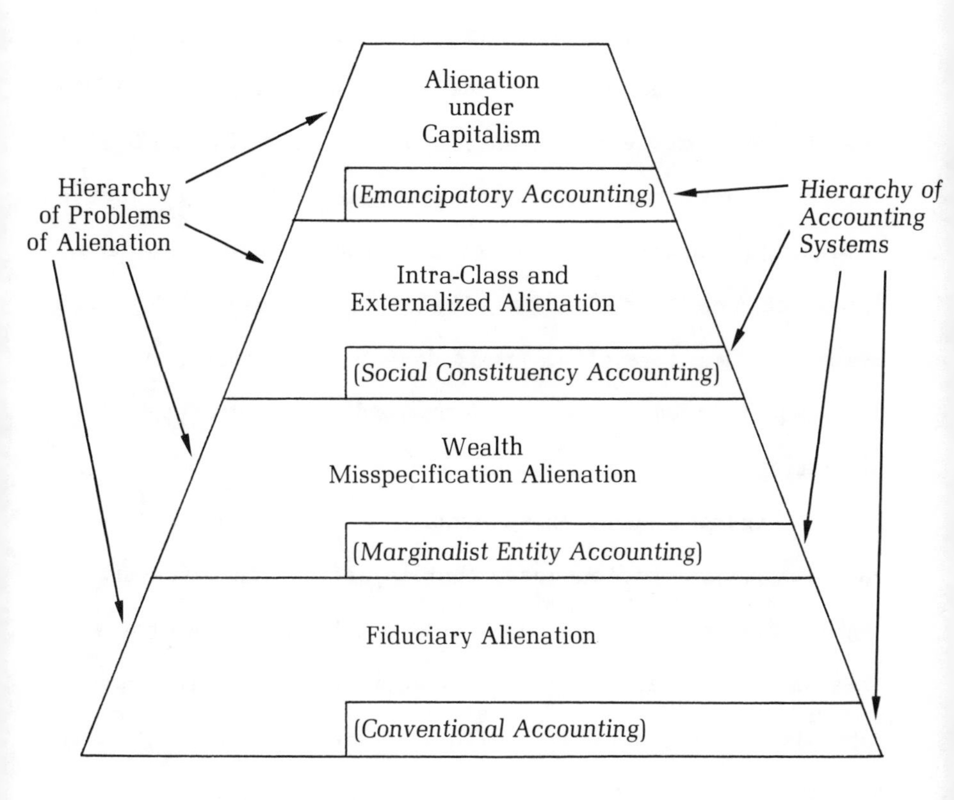

need to be developed and implemented. The aim here is not just to describe existing practice, but to delineate ways in which practice might be enhanced. The hypothetical accounting systems in Figure 3 are essential to this purpose. Our attention must be directed at clarifying the nature of the (alienation) problems that accounting—potentially as well as actually—helps resolve. This is the key to defining what "improvement" in accounting practice means, and, as we will see, Figure 3 will help us assess the degree of improvement that alternative accounting systems offer in terms of their "perceptiveness," "consciousness," or "sensitivity" to alienation. Figure 3 assists in this regard because it depicts an ascending scale of problems of alienation and a corresponding scale of potential accounting systems.

Figure 3 shows an accounting system corresponding to each level of consciousness, that is defined in terms of the degree of alienation that it perceives. As they stand however, these hypothetical accounting systems and their perceptual capabilities remain rather abstract. They can be made concrete by exploring a number of contemporary accounting controversies and scandals and showing how these contemporary problems fall into one of the four types of alienation shown in figures 2 and 3. The value of these figures and their underlying ideas will be tested, therefore, in terms of their ability to make sense out of current events, disputes, trends, developments, etc.

From an in-depth examination of each level of alienation, we will begin to see the kinds of accounting systems needed for detecting different levels of social alienation. Fiduciary Alienation will not be included in this discussion as it is—by definition—examined by conventional accounting, and the focus of this work is on those forms of alienation that escape the attention of the conventional system.

CONTROVERSIES OVER WEALTH MISSPECIFICATION ALIENATION

Alienation through wealth misspecification arises because conventional accounting measures fail to reflect the "real" economic value of a corporate entity as envisaged by the Marginalist Theory of Value. By "real" economic value, marginalists mean either the present value of the future stream of cash that is expected to be earned for the firm's shareholders, or the firm's current stock market value (itself serving as the capital market's evaluation of the shareholders' prospective cash flow). The present value and the stock market value are semi-independent measures of a firm's "real" economic value. The detailed problems with each need not concern us here. Both approaches have marginalist origins in utility theory, they both value alternatives by summing discounted prospects over time and assume that cash is a monotonically decreasing function of utility, and they both depend on subjective preferences and subjective expectations as to prospective cash flows and discount rates.

Because conventional accounting ignores the cash flow implications of many decisions, it encourages Wealth Misspecification Alienation. For instance, under FASB rules, research and development expenditures are treated as period expenses and, therefore, do not appear as assets on a firm's balance sheet under conventional accounting, even though such expenditures may produce substantial future earning and, therefore, represent a real addition to current wealth. Similarly, the wealth impact of employing superior (or inferior) management is rarely recorded in the conventional accounts, even though it may be crucial in valuing a company for a merger or takeover. (After a takeover or merger, such an item frequently does appear in the accounts as "goodwill.")

A popular pastime among accounting academics is to highlight the inability of conventional accounting to produce measures that accurately depict a marginalist version of income and wealth. We have termed it: Marginalist Entity Accounting, and it is quantified in terms of the present value of future cash flows). This shortcoming is illustrated in a multitude of textbooks and academic writings (see for example, Edwards and Bell, 1970; Parker and Harcourt, 1969; May, Muller, and Williams, 1975; Hendrickson, 1970). All of these tracts treat the Marginalist conception of value as a kind of theoretical ideal, and either offer policy proposals that supposedly would move accounting practice closer to that ideal, or otherwise justify existing accounting practice as "the best approximation" to the ideal.

Marginalist Value Theory has been influential in academic circles and has had considerable impact on the reporting practices of corporations. Currently, present value methods are used in valuing leases, pension liabilities, goodwill, fixed assets where payment is deferred, and oil and gas reserves. These are all examples of attempts to align conventional accounting practice with Marginalist principles, thereby reducing Wealth Misspecification Alienation. By producing more "realistic" estimates of the value to obtain an accurate report of corporate worth, Marginalism aims to reduce alienation by attaining an efficient allocation of social resources.

Numerous examples of Wealth Misspecification Alienation exists in contemporary accounting history. National Student Marketing (NSM) boosted its annual profits by exaggerating revenues and understating expenses. Appended to NSM's accounts was, what Andrew Tobias describes as, a "killer footnote" concerning the $3,754,103 profits included in the current period that referred to acquisitions after the year-end. Deferred product and start-up costs of $533,000, and the cost of pre-paid sales programs of $1,048,000 were both omitted from current expenses, and a large unbilled receivables item was included to inflate annual revenues. Even without hindsight, many Marginalist proponents would argue that these items distorted reality and increased alienation by failing to reflect the "real" Marginalist economic income. Similarly, it has been argued that the $2.2 billion accumulated deferred taxes, charged against the 1980 annual profits of public utilities, is a fictitious item because, in the view of many analysts, it is unlikely to materialize. Its effect is to understate accounting profits relative to Marginalist income, and to understate the wealth of the stockholder. To many observers, this understatement of profits was not an end in itself, but part of an attempt by public utilities to justify price increases using their certified financial statements as authority for their case. Apart from Wealth Misspecification, ultimately, this case illustrates a second form of alienation: Externalized Alienation, where managers and shareholders appropriate wealth from customers to themselves through price increases.

Wealth Misspecification Alienation arises because Conventional Accounting does not share the foresight attributed to Marginalist Entity Accounting. Yet, despite the widespread discussion of this form of alienation in the accounting literature, there are reasons to believe it to be one of the least important forms of alienation. This is so because this form of alienation and the Marginalist Entity System that "theoretically" perceives it, fails to include any explicit consideration of deleterious effects on those "outside" the corporation (i.e., externalities and intra-class competition). In giving undivided attention to misdescriptions of the "real" financial condition of corporations, academic accountants overlook the fact that the corporation is not a monolith, and does not exist in a social vacuum. The corporation is only an entity—"in theory"—and, as such, is a fiction—a reification—that masks the array of conflicting social interests that compose it. By insisting that the corporation be the working unit of analysis, Conventional Accounting and Marginalist Entity Accounting remove from the agenda the differential impact of accounting practices on the individual constituencies that make up the corporation. If wealth and income are only computed for the corporate entity, then the profits and losses between different fractions (of shareholders, for instance) go undetected. Yet, this was exactly the kind of misappropriation that was perpetrated at National Student Marketing. Some managers, insider traders, and directors--all acting as shareholders--made exorbitant profits by using accounting information to entice new shareholders to invest in overvalued companies. Recognition of the profits and losses accruing to various fractions of capital are indispensable to understanding what happened at National Student Marketing, yet, by focusing exclusively on the corporate entity, we obscure these conflicts and their origins from view.

The two accounting systems that remain to be considered in Figure 3 provide more comprehensive frameworks for recognizing alienation than Marginalist Entity Accounting. The latter views the problem of alienation as essentially "technical" and "procedural" (seeking rules for income determination and asset measurement, for example). Social Constituency Accounting and Emancipatory Accounting give explicit recognition to the social and political context. Social Constituency Accounting acknowledges social conflict within the restricted terminology of Marginalism. Yet, even with this rather narrow vocabulary, we can see how Conventional Accounting fails to adequately reflect the level of alienation. Emancipatory Accounting goes beyond social Constituency Accounting to encompass those appropriations through unequal exchanges that are inherent in Capitalism itself. Accounting reformers show even less perception and cognizance of this form of alienation than they do of the externalities revealed by Social Constituency Accounting.

CONTROVERSIES OVER INTRA-CLASS AND EXTERNALIZED ALIENATION

Introduction

The hypothetical Social Constituency Accounting shown in Figure 3 would surpass Marginalist and Conventional Accounting systems in its ability to comprehend alienation. Specifically, it admits two forms of alienation not considered before: Intra-Class Alienation and Externalized Alienation. In order to explore these types of alienation, the following discussion is organized into five sections, each section illustrating a different variant of these forms of social appropriation. The five sections deal with appropriations from (and, therefore, the alienation of) shareholders, local communities and neighborhoods, customers, and employees, and overseas nations.

Just as Marginalist Entity Accounting was found to be inadequate because it fails to perceive many of the social antinomies and conflicts surrounding corporate activity, so we will find that Social Constituency Accounting, with its neo-classical ideological foundations, also fails to provide a full account of the forces at work in real situations. Thus, the following discussions of Social Constituency Accounting concludes with a review of the inadequacies of this framework and leads to a consideration of Emancipatory Accounting Systems, as a possible resolution of the difficulties raised.

Unlike Marginalist and Conventional Accounting, Social

Constituency Accounting recognizes conflicts of interest, both within the corporation, and between the corporation and other interest groups. The latter conflicts of "side-effects" of corporate behavior are frequently referred to as "externalities." "Externalities" are the (usually negative) affects of corporate activities on the well-being of community members outside the corporation, where these community members are unable to obtain redress for these consequences through legal, contractual, or other means. Air, ground, and water pollution are common examples of externalities. They result from corporate activities where the costs are not impounded in the profit and loss calculations of the responsible firms, but are borne by those not otherwise associated with the corporation. Examples include the acid rain generated by the smokestacks in the mid-west that has been linked with the death of large quantities of fish and plant life in Canadian lakes; similar links have been posited between the lakes in Scandinavia and the industrial areas of Northern Europe. Love Canal is a dramatic example of externalities, in the form of psychological, physical, and social harms that have befallen members of that community as a result of the "economical" waste disposal practices of Hooker Chemicals in the 1950's.

Society may require corporations to take account of the externality effects on others. This may be done by fines, compensation payments, or even restricting the use of particularly harmful technologies. Whatever method is used, the result is the same: The externality is internalized or impounded in the cost and profit functions of the offending corporation, with the result that the anti-social (alienating) effects may be curtailed or mitigated. Externalities that are dealt with in this way we will call "Institutionalized Externalities." "Institutionalized" refers to the existence of social or legal processes for recognizing and impounding claims based on negative externalities.

In addition to forcing corporations to absorb negative externalities into their cost calculations, social processes also exist that enable corporations to impound positive externalities into their revenue calculations. Legal disputes over copyright or patent infringement are examples of conflicts over the property rights inherent in positive externalities. It is often difficult to establish who has proper legal title in such cases as in the current controversy over the right to record television and radio broadcasts. Corporations are not always required to impound their negative externalities into their cost functions. Such cases are termed here, "Non-Institutionalized Externalities." Examples of Non-Institutionalized Externalities include the injury and loss of life among citizens of some Third World countries who have purchased over-the-counter, poorly described, and extremely powerful drugs (e.g. steroids) supplied by European and U.S.-based pharmaceutical multinationals seeking to dispose of their excess production. Another example relates to the infants in countries who have died because Nestle promoted the sale of concentrated milk without giving adequate information to mothers about the conditions under which the product should be used. In this case, Nestle sued a Swiss group of church and other activists for libel. However, even the highly conservative, pro-business Swiss courts dismissed seven out of eight of the charges.

In general, few practical legal remedies are available to the victims of such tragic affairs; the only way in which these negative externalities have been imposed on the cost functions of multinationals has been by increasing their public relations costs and through "informal" social processes (e.g. public boycotts and sanctions).

No hard and fast line divides Institutionalized from Non-Institutionalized Externalities in that an externality that is not impounded at one point of time may become impounded at a later date, and vice versa. For instance, while there was some medical evidence in the 1950's that pointed to the harmful affects of toxic waste, it is unlikely that the courts would have supported a financial claim against chemical firms in that early period. Such externalities are now widely recognized by the courts. We cannot assume, however, an uninterrupted progression whereby government and the courts will require corporations to recognize a greater proportion of the externalities that result from their behavior. An example was provided recently by Manville Corporation who, facing millions of dollars of legal claims by sixteen thousand workers suffering from asbestos-related diseases, has filed for bankruptcy under Chapter 11 (New York Times, December 10th, 1982). The effect of filing for bankruptcy was, "to freeze all claims and not spend a dime defending them" (ibid). According to the New York Times, business has been better than usual for Manville and its stockholders: since filing the claim for bankruptcy, Manville's share price rose from 4.5 to 9.5 between August 27th and December 9th 1982.

In many ways, it is more helpful to view conflict over externalities (positive and negative) as merely a further instance of the struggle over the distribution of income of wealth. Viewed in this fashion, there is no fundamental difference between a company that attempts to "disown" millions of dollars of legal claims due to asbestos poisoning, and a firm that successfully disposes of its pension obligations to employees (as in the Harvester Company case that we will consider subsequently). Both situations are identical insofar as they both exemplify a struggle between different social constituencies over the distribution of income; a struggle in which accounting plays an important and substantial part.

Fromgeneral considerations as to the nature of Intra-Class and Externalized Alienation, we can now examine a number of current controversies. These are discussed under five headings: alienation of corporate shareholders; the local community; customers; employees, and Third World countries. The inadequacies of the concept of Inter-Class and Externalized alienation are then reviewed by way of an introduction to the final section (on Alienation under capitalism).

Appropriation from Shareholders

Appropriations from shareholders by management (or other shareholder groups) form the gist of many controversies surrounding conventional accounting practice. Yet, as we have seen, because of the application of the Entity Principle, the full impact of these "unequal exchanges" has been obscured, with the consequence that exposure and criticism of appropriative practices have been more muted than they might have been. Examples of the appropriation of shareholders funds are manifold: Ponzi schemes are classic examples of mechanisms for appropriating shareholders' wealth. Recent examples of Ponzi schemes include the Homestake case and S-J Minerals affair. While accounting information did not play a central role in enticing investors to part with $130 million to Home-stake and

$20 million to S-J Minerals, these cases do highlight the way misleading information can create false expectations among investors and encourage them to part with their money. The losses (externalities) suffered by investors in National Student Marketing (NSM) and Slater Walker Ltd. (UK) are further instances of appropriations from shareholders by management (Intra-Class Alienation). Some investors in NSM, who purchased at around $140 per share, watched their holdings fall to an all-time low of $3.50. Those who held out to the company's liquidation in late 1980, would have received approximately $26 per share (before stock splits)--a total possible loss of $114 per unit (New York Times, December 11th, 1980, p. 56.) Such losses (and profits) were the result of trading between shareholders and, as such, they went unrecognized in the firm's reports because, at the level of the accounting entity, all losses are matched by gains of equal value.

The fact that directors and senior executives are legally obliged to report share dealings in their employer companies is an acknowledgment that not all shareholders are equal, and that there are occasions when abandonment of the Entity Principle is justified. But this would be only a mild relaxation in the accountant's near universal emphasis on the corporate entity, and would do little to redirect the otherwise obsessive search for more precise measures of the value of assets, liabilities, and profits of the reified corporate aggregate. Jim Slater, the managing director of Slater Walker, ridiculed the emphasis on paper profits in bragging that his company's objective was to "make money, not things." He showed the folly of not seeing the links between accounting information, shareholder expectations, and the "massaging" of share prices. High personal gains were obtained for himself and his fellow directors, not by manufacturing and selling, but my manipulating share prices using the funds that clients had deposited with Slater Walker Ltd.

Jim Slater appreciated only too well the potential conflict of interest between 'inside' and 'outside' shareholders. Cortes Randell of National Student Marketing, whose personal fortune at one time reached $3 million, also showed good insight into the role that accounting income figures could play in redistributing wealth from one group of shareholders to another.

One can only surmise the reason why accounting theorists have retained the Entity Assumption and resisted attending to the potential conflicts of interest that exists between different fractions of capital. Possibly, accountants fear that by focusing on such conflicts, they might discredit capital market pursuits as "unproductive speculation;" a view already widely held in some circles.

Appropriations from the Community

By November 1981, it was estimated that clean-up and relocation efforts arising from the Love Canal tragedy, had cost state and federal authorities $95 million. This was separate from the $2.65 billion in legal claims that are currently being brough against the company (The Progressive, November, 1981, pp. 35-42.) Moreover, some commentators have suggested that Love Canal was one of Hooker's best-managed operations (ibid). To date, Hooker Chemicals and its parent firm, Occidental Petroleum, have been prosecuted in Florida, Michigan, California, and New York. (Ibid; p. 42; Wall Street Journal, Sept. 29th, 1981, p. 56.) In Lathrop, California, twenty-eight workers have filed a suit against Hooker charging that the chemicals they worked with caused sterility. In New York State, Hooker was fined $500,000 for dumping toxic material on a landfill next to the Gruman Aerospace Plant. It is now believed that Gruman workers unknowingly drank contaminated water for years and two drinking water wells have since been closed after traces of vc and pvc were found (ibid, p. 39.) In Taft, Louisiana, contractors who were hired by Hooker to extend the firm's plant sued the company, claiming that exposure to chlorine had left them sterile, impotent and without a sense of taste and smell. Hooker settled out-of-court for amounts ranging from $7,000 to $250,000. In White Lake, Michigan,

Hooker dumped over 20,000 barrels on a site behind their own plant. Seepage has polluted the lake and killed large numbers of fish. The State of Michigan took the company to court in 1979 and, in an out-of-court settlement, the company agreed to pay for the clean-up (estimated to be close to $20 million) and more than $1 million more in penalties.

By focusing on costs to the corporate entity, accounting practice systematically excludes costs that corporations may "externalize" and impose on other members of the community. Even when these costs are internalized (through fines, out-of-court settlements, special levies and taxes, etc.) accountants still become parties to a deception as to what the costs really mean. The financial awards by the courts are usually taken by accountants as "the last word" on valuing externalities; with the result that the appropriateness of valuations in legal decisions is rarely questioned, despite considerable evidence of arbitrary and inconsistent behavior by the courts. A moment's reflection on the immensely complex nature of most problems brought before the courts, and the processes by which they arrive at a judgment, confirms this point. In one case--involving, not pollution, but the police shooting of a deaf mute child who ran away from suspicious circumstances and failed to respond to calls to halt--the boy's parents were awarded $10. The award was a negligible amount because the court based it on the expected earnings capacity of deaf mutes.

The externalities that conventional accounting overlooks are intergenerational as well as cross-sectional. This is especially the case in relation to pollution where there has been a tendency to postpone confronting major environmental problems; a tendency that is reinforced by the accounting practice of only recognizing environmental costs when the courts or state impose a liability on the corporation. EPA official Douglas Costle illustrates how costs are "pushed into the next generation" with regard to the pollution of the James River with Kepone. The culprit in this case was the Life Science Products Co. in Hopwell, Virginia, in 1975 (New York Times, September 27th, 1980, p. 69.) The original pollution could have been cleaned up at a cost of $250,000, but the company delayed and has since paid out $13 million in damages claims. Now, experts estimate, it will cost at least $2 billion to clean up the river. "In a misguided sense of thrift, we save ourselves broke," contends Costle (ibid). Would this pollution have been averted if the firm's auditors had insisted that a liability be recognized once management had decided to release the Kapone?

Equally serious, as an example of intergenerational "wealth" transfers, is the pollution and long-term diminution of the vast underground water reservoirs (aquifers) that extend under several states. Americans obtain over half of their drinking water from these underground sources of "fossil water" that has taken over 25,000 years to accumulate (New York Times, December 29, 1980). Because this water is not open to the sunlight and moves very little, agricultural and other toxins take much longer to decompose than otherwise would be the case. Moreover, the usage of this water is well in excess of the replacement rate in many parts of the country. In parts of California, the water table has been so lowered by intensive irrigation that the land has settled thirty feet in places. Overall, in the wet East, a significant 12 percent of the water used has not been returned to the aquifers; in the arid West, the quantity was a staggering 52%.

We have touched on all but a small sample of intergenerational and intracommunal appropriations and the heightened levels of alienation that ensue. Further examples will arise in subsequent discussions; including the loan liabilities that the U.S. government has recently underwritten in order to provide support for U.S. banks, and the growing employee pension burden that private companies have imposed on the public purse. These cases involve a colossal redistribution of income from the community to private corporations. We will see that accounting practice was a party to this appropriative exercise in its neglect of the social impact of corporate activities.

Appropriations From Customers

Excessive prices charged by public utilities are appropriations in that they constitute unequal exchanges. These exchanges are unequal, not only in the classical theory sense of an exchange of unequal amounts of embodied labor time, but also in relation to the norms of competitive capitalism where prices are "reasonable" only if they conform to those that would prevail in long-run, competitive conditions. Whatever criterion we use to adjudge whether public utility prices are "excessive," if accounting practices are used in setting exorbitant prices, then part of the responsibility for the appropriation and exploitation falls on the accounting community.

A cost-plus-profit formula is often used in establishing the prices of gas, water, telephone and other utility services, and these costs are usually included in an item called "deferred taxation." In 1975, deferred taxation for the 150 largest companies amounted to approximately $1.5 billion. American Telephone and Telegraph had accumulated $11.3 billion in deferred taxation by the end of 1978, and this was increasing by an estimated $2.4 billion each year.

Deferred taxation is an expense that is anticipated rather than actually paid during the accounting period. If the expense never materializes then, insofar as this item has been included in the cost-plus-utility rate fixing, then customers redistributive influence may be no less significant. Indeed, the wave of mergers and takeovers in the early 1980's, and the greater concentration in ownership and control that this has brought about, has increased the impact of accounting on pricing and income distribution. In stark contrast to the popular mythology of accountants as passive bookkeepers and "technicians," this scenario suggests a prominent role for accounting in social choices: As an architect of redistributive policies that are executed on behalf of corporations. Such an awesome responsibility might—one would have thought—have stung accountants into a fundamental re-examination of the soundness of their practices. The fact that such a self-examination is not forthcoming is not surprising in the light of the allegiances and dependencies of accounting firms and accounting academics.

Appropriations From Employees

The employee pension expense exemplifies the way accounting fabrications have expropriated employee income. Private corporations, city governments, federal, state, and local authorities, have all indulged in extravagant promises of pension benefits to employees, without being required to provide for these commitments in any comprehensive and systematic way. Conventional accounting treats the pension benefits that an employee earns in the current period as a charge against current income, even though the pension may not be payable for twenty or thirty years hence. The difficulty is in estimating the current cost of future payments. In addition to this difficulty, accounting rules permit corporations and other institutions to systematically understate this current cost by not requiring them to set aside finds now to provide for the future payment. The result is to allow corporations to have unfunded liabilities with the consequence that the firm's net income for the current period may be grossly overstated. Liabilities of corporations with some of the largest unfunded pension liabilities in 1979 and 1980 are shown in Table 1.

An unfunded pension liability is one where no investments have been made to provide liability when it falls due. Moreover, under conventional accounting, unfunded liabilities are not usually shown as liabilities in the accounts; they are only footnoted. Furthermore, the unfunded figures in the above table understate the magnitude of the liability because they only refer to vested benefits (benefits that the corporation is legally obligated to pay). There are many additional costs, not included in the above, that the employees have already earned but will only become legal entitlements in the future, when a period of service has been completed, or some other conditions of employment have been

TABLE 1

UNFUNDED PENSION LIABILITIES OF MAJOR CORPORATIONS

IN 1979 AND 1980 *

Unfunded Vested
Pension Benefits: Million of dollars

COMPANY	1979	1980	% OF NET WORTH
General Motors	$6,100	$4,085	32%
Ford Motor	1,920	-0-	18%
Chrysler	1,200	1,275	66%
Bethlehem Steel	1,191	420	46%
U.S. Steel	1,000	-0-	20%
Lockheed	391	-0-	117%
LTV	624	62	87%
National Steel	660	104	47%

---

* from several sources quoted in the preceding text.

fulfilled. In addition, the above figures are only rough estimates of the present cost of the future vested liabilities. Not only are these amounts very difficult to estimate, but corporations have shown little hesitation in using loopholes in the accounting rules to present their performance in the most favorable light (Business Week, August 25th, 1980, pp. 94-5; Duns Review, May 1981, pp. 78-82.)

The failure of accounting practice to insist on a more realistic assessment of a corporation's pension obligations has serious consequences. By understating the current pension expense, current profits are overstated and may be distributed as dividends, rather than being retained in the firm to meet the pension obligation when it falls due. When corporations are unable to meet their pension commitments, it will be employees, other corporations, and the state, who are frequently the losers. Recently, International Harvester Co. was accused of dumping $45 million of pension liabilities into the Pension Benefit Guarantee Corporation (PBGC). The PBGC is financed by private companies whose pension plans it guarantees; thus, other companies eventually bear the cost of underfunded pension plans that fold. Currently, the PBGC is suing Harvester on the grounds that the sale of Evirodyne to Wisconsin Steel amounted to a fraud intended to spare Harvester a pension debt of $86.2 million (Wall Street Journal, Tuesday, December 7th, 1982).

Underfunding of pension obligations is as rampant in the state and local government sectors as it is in the private sector. There are some 6,000 state and local pension plans that are reputably ill-managed and have $300 billion in unfunded liabilities (Los Angeles Times, November 19th, 1978, Section 5, p. 5.) As of 1979, the Fire and Police Pension Fund in Los Angeles was underfunded by $2 billion. As of 1979, the pension plan for the New York fire department had obligations in the form of vested benefits valued at $1.5 billion and pension assets of only $0.5 billion (Wall Street Journal, February 26th, 1979). It was anticipated that this fund would be stripped of its assets within a decade (ibid).

Appropriations Between Nation States

The events preceding the passage of the Foreign Corrupt Practices Act in the United States highlight the detrimental impact of externalities and appropriative behavior at the international level. In the mid-1970's, a series of bribery scandals were uncovered involving U.S.-based multinationals and senior officials, military personnel and politicians of foreign governments. These scandals destabilized the governments of Japan, South Korea, the Netherlands, Indonesia, and other nations. Senate hearings in 1975-76 revealed that Lockheed had paid more than $106 million in secret "commissions" to promote foreign sales, including $7 million to a well-connected Japanese agent who was also head of a right-wing youth movement. These payments were additional to those made to Mr. Tanaka, who was once Japan's prime minister and one of that country's most influential politicians (and remains so even to this day). Mr. Tanaka was forced to step down from office amid accusations that he accepted a $2.5 million bribe from Lockheed. Tanaka's trial droned on for six years; he was convicted in 1983—an event that precipitated a general election and a crisis for the Japanese government that continues to this day (Forbes, January 31st, 1983, p. 74.) Lockheed also made large secret payments to Prince Bernhard of the Netherlands to influence his recommendations as Inspector General of the Armed Forces concerning fighter-plane purchases by the Dutch government. The scandal that ensued in Holland nearly led to the deposal of the Dutch Royal family. In Italy, Exxon funneled more than $50 million to Italian political parties and cabinet members to buy favorable tax and energy legislation (New York Times, June 8th, 1981).

These scandals led Congress to pass the Foreign Corrupt Practices Act in 1977, making it illegal to pay bribes to foreign government officials. As a result of the Act, corporations are required to disclose of questionable payments that they had made previously and, as a result of these revelations, 527 firms were cited by the SEC (Newsweek, February

19th 1979). In addition to Exxon and Lockheed, it was revealed that questionable payments had been made by Boeing ($500 million), General Tire and Rubber ($41 million) Northrop ($34 million), and many others.

The various debates surrounding the Foreign Corrupt Practices Act are instructive as to the externalities involved and the likelihood that these forms of alienation might rebound on American business interests. During the Senate hearings, Senator Church noted that, "Morality in the business community is not our responsibility, nor is enforcing the law in other lands. What this government and this Congress must concern itself with are the very real and serious political and economic consequences that spreading corruption can have for U.S. interests both at home and abroad." (New York Times, June 8th).

Senator Church's concerns lay, not with the detrimental effects of bribery and corruption on the citizens of foreign states, but with the possibility that bribery might damage American interests to an extent that far exceeds any benefits derived. "The country would have been better off if Lockheed hadn't paid bribes to Japan," said Lindy Marinaccio, an aide to Senator Proxmire, adding, "The country is big enough to forgo the sale of several Lockheed airplanes."

The precarious state of the world banking system provides one of the most dramatic illustrations of the damage that may result from accounting myopia regarding externalities. Time Magazine estimates that in January 1983, a gargantuan debt of $706 billion was owed to banks, governments, and international financial institutions around the world by a group of deeply troubled developing and Eastern bloc countries (Time, January 10th, 1983). Felix Rohatyn, senior partner of the Lazard Freres investment bank, who organized some of the largest corporate mergers in the 1970's, has estimated that some $500 billion of the amount owed by developing and Eastern bloc European loans are being recycled at increasingly higher interest rates and will never be repaid (New York Review of Books, November, 1982; The Progressive, February, 1983, p. 23.)

The financial chaos predicted by Rohatyn is underscored by a recent series of unexpected shocks to the world financial system. Ever since Poland defaulted in March 1981 with a debt of $21 billion, the danger signals have been flying. In August 1982, Mexico announced that it could not meet interest payments on its debt of $81 billion; Brazil followed soon after with a declaration that it could not make any further payments towards its $40 billion loans. Argentina has also defaulted on payments towards its $40 billion loans. These trends were confirmed by an International Monetary Fund report that in 1981, 32 countries were in arrears with their debts compared with 15 countries in 1975 (Time, January 10th, 1983, p. 42.)

The situation looks serious if doubtful loans are

related to the shareholders equity which, coupled with loss loan reserves, can be thought of what a bank would have left if it paid off its depositors and creditors. Chemical Bank, for instance, has loans of $1.5 billion outstanding to Mexico and Argentina, and this represents 92% of shareholder equity. Equivalent ratios for Chase Manhattan and Citicorp are 77% and 95%, respectively. Altogether, the nine largest U.S. banks have loaned out about 130% of their equity to Mexico, Brazil, and Argentina.

The financial difficulties of some Eastern block and developing countries has been a matter of public discussion for some years now; critics ask why banks did not anticipate this situation and why accounting reports failed to register the doubtful value of loans shown as assets on the bank's balance sheets. Indeed, the nine largest banks have set aside a total of 3.6 billion in loss-loan reserves; but this amounts to only 12% of the total owed by Mexico, Argentina, and Brazil. The behavior of the banks in this affair has been attributed to their fear of precipitating a collapse; it is much easier to advance more money to a borrower in difficulty, in the hope that matters will improve, than it is to call a halt that may have chilling repercussions for the world financial system. The modest accounting provisions for loan-losses suggests that the auditors of banks were accomplices in this deception.

By masking the deteriorating financial position of U.S. banks, accounting practice has fostered financial irresponsibility and mismanagement among both borrowers and lenders. Many observers fear that the "cost" of this incompetence will not fall on the banking corporations. If the treatment of Poland and Argentina is indicative, then it seems that the U.S. government is willing to pump money into the system to keep U.S. banks afloat. The financial burden of this solution will not fall on the banks however, but will eventually be imposed on U.S. citizens through inflationary pressures and the devaluation of their currency, culminating in a transfer of U.S. wealth into the hands of foreign dollar holders. The inflationary impact of this solution could be more substantial than anything seen previously: Felix Rohatyn's assessment is that $500 billion may never be repaid, this amounts to $2,500 per capita for U.S. citizens--a substantial amount that translates into a lower quality of life and greater alienation for the individual.

Limitations of the Social Constituency Accountancy Perspective

The Social Constituency view suffers from one major theoretical flaw: Its definition of alienation is ambiguous. The source of the difficulty lies with the notion of an externality which, largely because of its Marginalist derivations, is a subjective and arbitrary concept. Consider the case of Love Canal. We assume that, if the courts recognize claims of the local citizens against the company, then an externality exists, and the legal damages reflect the measure of the alienation involved. Suppose, however, that the Love Canal citizens had brought their action in the 1950's and had been unsuccessful. Are we to conclude that no alienation existed in the 1950's but it did in the 1980's? The situation becomes even more ambiguous if we believe that, had accountants been more concerned about social issues in the 1950's, legal conventions might have changes to recognize the legitimacy of legal claims--and therefore the presence of alienation.

The source of the ambiguity lies in valuing what is suffered or given up. An externality clearly exists if toxic waste dumping has a deleterious effect on some members of the community. But what if the cost of disposal was so prohibitive as to have drastic repercussions on the material well-being of all parties concerned. Then we might conclude that no externality is involved, and that "pollution with plastics," is far more desirable than "no pollution and no plastic," even for the residents of Love Canal.

We can conclude from the above that, whenever an externality is said to exist, it is implied that a superior state of affairs is forgone, and this provides the benchmark against which to measure the externality. If a firm pollutes a river, fishermen suffer externalities because an unpolluted river is implicitly assumed to be the next best available alternative that is forgone. When Lockheed bribed the prime minister of Japan, an externality was said to exist because it was implicitly assumed that "business without bribes" was the possibility forgone.

Unfortunately, there is no discussion in the theory of externalities (which is part of marginalism) as to how to systematically determine which possibilities are forgone, or how to value them, i.e., the opportunity cost. Alternatives are either "pregiven" or "subjectively determined"; they are not enumerated by the theory itself. This theoretical lacunae allows certain biases to affect the set of alternatives that are contemplated and therefore the assessment as to whether an externality exists or not. For instance, on what grounds may we conclude that the only options available to Love Canal residents are, "pollution with plastics" and "no pollution, no plastics?"

The following section on Emancipatory Accounting and "capitalist alienation" attempts to address these difficulties. In particular, it defines alienation "objectively" (rather than subjectively) in terms of the "alternatives" that are admitted under capitalism, and shows that all capitalist possibilities are alienating, relative to a non-exploitative social order. The discussion argues that the existence and magnitude of alienating externalities are not dependent on a "pregiven" or arbitrarily assumed set of opportunities forgone, but on "objective" social structural conditions that are inherently alienating.

Emancipatory Accounting and Capitalist Alienation

What distinguishes capitalism, as a social system, is its class structure and the form that class conflict assumes. Capitalists and laborers form the two major divisions under capitalism in that each citizen obtains the means of subsistence either by working, or through the ownership of property, or through some combination of the two. The subsistence received by labor is essential for reproducing the worker and therefore the continuance of production. Profits, in contrast, do not help reproduce the productive process because capitalists--qua capitalists--make no personal contribution to production. In this very specific sense, capitalists appropriate from the production process without giving anything in return; their property income is not a material relation in that it is not indispensable for production to occur, but a social relation that is specific to Capitalism.

Capitalist alienation is expressed in two forms; in the appropriation of the value created by labor which is consumed by property owners; and in the structure of the division of labor itself. These two forms of alienation are sometimes called social alienation and subjective alienation, respectively. The Labor Theory of Value of Smith, Ricardo, and Marx provided a way of identifying social alienation. Marx showed that, what Ricardo mistakenly took to be discrepancies in the Law of Value (differences between labor time ratios and exchangeable values), was, in fact, a measure of the appropriation by capital from labor. But while appropriation through unequal exchange is an important part of human alienation under Capitalism, it does not account for all types of alienation. The division of labor itself assumes a distorted and "unproductive" form because it acts as a vehicle for perpetuating unequal social relations of capitalism. In particular, the enforcement of returns to property, and securing a profit return, gives a special character to the division of labor. The police and the military represent a considerable coercive power in supporting property entitlements; the courts expend substantial human talents and energies in the preservation of property rights, and ideological support is provided by an array of religious, educational, media, and other belief-forming institutions. In addition to changing the array of tasks contained within the division of labor, capitalist relations distort the composition of individual tasks: Teachers not only teach, they also discipline; hospitals not only heal, they also incarcerate those who do not fit in; managers do not just manage things they also manage people, etc.

"Emancipatory Accounting" includes information systems that are cognizant of the alienating foundations of Capitalism, and therefore exhibits a far greater comprehension of alienation than any of the other accountability systems discussed previously. The superior critical potential of Emancipatory Accounting is illustrated by examining contemporary events, particularly where private and public interests come into conflict. For instance, given the market imperative, it would be irrational for Hooker Chemicals, or any other producer of toxic waste, to do anything other than minimize costs of disposal (including any litigation costs). Nor can we expect firms like Slater Walker, National Student Marketing, and S-J Minerals, to concern themselves with damaging public confidence in savings and investment. The market imperative driving institutions of capitalism is to make profits and adopt any political, social or accounting device at its disposal to realize that aim. This behavior is an inevitable consequence of organizing an economy according to the priorities, rights, duties and obligations of property relations and wage labor.

The logic of capitalist institutions to obey the market imperative does not mean that accountants should simply aid and abet them in their mission. Unfortunately, the reality is that accountants have consistently viewed social conflict from a corporatist perspective, a viewpoint that ignores dysfunctionalities that are perceived even by marginalist ideology.

The corporatist affiliations of accountants raise serious doubts about the impartiality of the profession and the social relevance of accounting reports. Accounting measures of profit and wealth have little to do with social efficiency and productivity; rather, they are indices of expropriation and social alienation. In the light of this, accountants may want to reassess their own work and the way that the subject is presently constructed. Accountants do not need to give unquestioning allegiance to corporations; the certification requirement imposed by the Securities Acts established a public responsibility for auditors that transcends any "private" relationship between auditor and client. While some may feel that the profession has failed in its public charge, the responsibility is still treated by many with the utmost seriousness.

What is to be done? The last section examines this question in the light of the prior discussions. Our three contributors all take a broader view of the accounting problematic than that entailed by a corporatist perspective. In the remaining section, I will attempt to show the fundamental ways in which our contributors differ, between themselves, and in relation to the conventional perspective of accounting.

A Classification of Critical Accounting Literature

Previously, contemporary accounting was contrasted with three alternative accounting systems: Marginalist Entity Accounting, Social Constituency Accounting, and Emancipatory Accounting. We saw that, compared with contemporary accounting, these three hypothetical perspectives provided insights into problems of alienation emanating from corporate activity.

Figure 3 (presented earlier), together with the discussion of contemporary controversies, indicates what might be done to reduce the alienating effects of accounting theory and practice. We saw that the notion of a corporate entity is a fiction and that, in reality, this "entity" is afflicted by numerous social antagonisms and antinomies. Intra-Class and Externalized Alienation draws attention to the ways corporations may create havoc beyond their boundaries. The fact that externalities may not be legally recognized (non-institutionalized) in no way diminishes their significance from a socio-economic viewpoint. Capitalist Alienation acknowledges the unstable tendencies that are inherent within capitalism itself. These instabilities are the source of much of the rapacious and exploitative behavior expressed at the other two levels of alienation (externalizing costs, for instance). Only with a perspective that reveals capitalism in socially relative terms will accountants be able to recognize the sources and manifestations of alienation.

The above considerations are not merely "academic" or "abstract;" they have immense practical importance and have already been explored in a number of preliminary ways. For example, Harold Tyler, the judge who sentenced the two CPA's who audited NSM, concluded that too many people in the accounting profession exhibited, "Some sort of myopia as to what is really the public responsibility of someone who performs services as a public servant." Tyler's comment asserts the existence of a public interest that is not the same as private interests, and that public accountants have a responsibility to both discern and satisfy the public interest.

Our three contributors have offered various suggestions for expanding the horizons of accounting. These suggestions may be examined in relation to Figure 2, which aspires to provide a "total picture" of the variety of problems confronting accountants. All three contributors accept without question the role of accounting in combating Fiduciary Alienation and Wealth Misspecification Alienation. Moreover, in their different ways, our contributors also envisage a limited role for corporate accountability that extends to the third level of alienation in Figure 2: Intra-Class and Externalized Alienation. Intra-Class Alienation (conflicts within the shareholder class) has long been an item of concern in the accounting literature. The informational advantages enjoyed by inside shareholders, who use their privileged managerial positions to profit from other, less well-informed investors, are cited by Briloff and Sporkin in their references to Drysdale Securities, Penn Square, National Student Marketing, and Grant Stores. These two writers also envisage a need for corporate accountability in the area of Externalized Alienation, and here they are joined by Lindblom. Briloff refers to Lockheed's involvement in foreign corrupt practices while Sporkin uses environmental pollution as an example that justifies accountability for Externalized Alienation. Interestingly, in discussion, Sporkin expounds the rationale for this broader notion of accountability in terms of a simple extension of protecting shareholder interests rather than some lofty ideals pertaining to the public interest. He commends this rationale, not on "logical" or "intellectual" grounds, but in terms of political expediency; that Congress would only tolerate pollution regulations that were couched in terms of the interests of capital.

It is unclear whether Sporkin and Briloff would support curbs on Externalized Alienation (e.g. corruption, pollution) if no adverse repercussions were expected to befall shareholders, or if shareholders were likely to profit from externalizing costs. These two authors rely on the assumption that shareholders will always be eventually "punished"—through the courts, or the market place--if a corporation "misbehaves" by externalizing costs. But the more general case is likely to be that where shareholders profit from externalizing costs, and in this case we lack a persuasive argument from either Briloff or Sporkin that shows why such behavior is undesirable and should be curtailed. Personally, I have little doubt that both authors would support greater corporate accountability in such circumstances. This, however, is not my point: In matters of public policy we require proposals to be sustained by arguments that go beyond invective and political expediency; we need to discuss the adversary interests that may be affected by corporate decisions so that we may decide which side we are on.

Lindblom's contribution to the above discussion is very different from that of either Sporkin or Briloff. From the outset, he argues that there is a need to control large corporations, that market pressures provide insufficient controls over major decisions such as plant location and pollution, and that as no one today would seriously contemplate benevolent despotism as an adequate political system, why should we delegate extensive power and autonomy to nonelected corporate executives? Conflicts of interest are openly acknowledged in Lindblom's analysis (in contrast to Sporkin's more discrete, "political" approach, for example). The latter assigns paramount importance to the shareholders interest and attempts to argue that externalities will usually rebound on those interests.

Accordingly, if one wished to situate our three contributors in the "big picture" of corporate alienation (Figure 2), all three would occupy the first two levels of Fiduciary and Wealth Misspecification Alienation, and would only partly occupy Intra-Class and Externalized Alienation.

There is, however, a forth level of alienation, pertaining to capitalist social relations, that is largely untouched by the three contributors. Lindblom most closely approaches this form of alienation in discussing the democratization of corporate decision-making. Apart from this, the three perspectives tend to be politically voluntaristic in that they assume that problems can be remedied by a simple correction: They do not address the social circumstances sustaining the current maldistribution of power that endows corporate executives with so much authority. For Lindblom, the situation will be corrected once citizens--and accountants--realize that corporations too must be incorporated within politico-democratic processes. Briloff and Sporkin would appear to subscribe to even more voluntaristic positions by defining problems in the individualistic terms of the immoral misbehavior of managers. (The implication of this argument being that the source of corporate alienation lies exclusively with individual managers and not within the structure of circumstances in which firms and managers operate.)

Capitalist Alienation refers to social structural conditions of inequality that are integral to capitalist society. These conditions refer to relations between social members and their rights and entitlements regarding life-sustaining property and tools of production. The instability engendered by these structural conditions is not explicitly considered by the three contributors, either as the source of the alienation considered in their analysis, or as a form of alienation in its own right. Lindblom has explored such considerations elsewhere, however, the specific links to accounting and corporate accountability still need to be spelled out.

At the outset of this book, I noted that there seemed little point in writing a review that was simply a rehash of what was being reviewed. In discharging my reviewers responsibilities, I hope that our three contributors will excuse what, at times, may have been excessive critical enthusiasm aimed, not so much as their work, but at "liberal" theoretical tendencies found elsewhere in the accounting and management literature. I am very much aware that Professors Briloff, Lindblom, and Stanley Sporkin are among the most effective exponents of a new approach to accounting and accountability.

My own contribution is a very modest one: Accounting

theorists cannot hope to progress without incorporating an analysis of capitalism and its alienating propensities. Appeals for greater individual honesty and integrity by accountants are important but will be of little consequence without also addressing the socio-environment that galvanizes acquisitive and competitive behavior.

BIBLIOGRAPHY

Braverman, H. Labor And Monopoly Capital. Monthly Review Press, New York, 1974.

Briloff, Abraham. Unaccountable Accounting. Harper and Row, New York, 1972.

Briloff, Abraham. More Debits Than Credits. Harper and Row, New York, 1976.

Briloff, Abraham. The Truth About Corporate Accounting. Harper and Row, New York, 1981.

Dobb, Maurice. Political Economy And Capitalism: Some Essays in Economic Tradition. London, Routledge, and Kegan Paul, London, 1937.

Dobb, Maurice. Studies in the Development of Capitalism. International Publishers, New York, 1963, 2nd ed.

Dobb, Maurice. Theories of Value and Income Distribution Since Adam Smith: Ideology and Economic Theory. Cambridge University Press, Cambridge, 1973.

Edwards, R. S. and Bell, P. The Theory and Measurement of Business Income. University of California Press, Berkeley, 1961.

Elson, Diane. "The Value Theory of Labour." Diane Elson, ed., Value: The Representation of Labour in Capitalism. CSE and Humanities Press, London, 1979.

Embree, J. Sauye Mura: A Japanese Village. Routledge and Kegan Paul, London, 1946.

Habermas, J. Toward A Rational Society: Student Protest, Science and Politics. Beacon Press, Boston, 1968.

Harcourt, G. C. Some Cambridge Controversies in the Theory of Capital. Cambridge University Press, Cambridge, 1972.

Hendrickson, E. A. Accounting Theory. Richard D. Irwin, Homewood, Illinois, 1970.

Hicks, John. Capital and Growth. Oxford University Press, Oxford, 1965.

Kregel, J. The Reconstruction of Political Economy: An Introduction to Post-Keynsian Economics. Macmillan, London, 1975, 2nd ed.

Kregel, J. A. Theory of Capital. Macmillan Studies in Economics, Macmillan, London, 1976.

Lekachman, Robert A History of Economic Ideas. McGraw Hill, New York, 1976.

Lukacs, G. History and Class Consciousness Studies in Marxist Dialectics. R. Livingstone, trans., London, 1971.

May, R. T., Mueller, G. and Williams T. A New Introduction to Financial Accounting. Prentice Hall, Englewood Cliffs, N. J., 1975.

Mandel, Ernest. Introduction to Marxist Economic Theory. Pathfinder Press, New York, 1970.

Marcuse, H. Some Dimensional Man. Beacon Press, New York, 1964.

Marx, K. The Poverty of Philosophy. Progress Publishers, Moscow, 1955.

Meek, Ronald, L. Smith, Marx and After. London, Chapman and Hall, 1977.

Meek, Ronald. Studies in the Labor Theory of Value. Monthly Review Press, New York, 1975, 2nd ed.

Morton, A. L. A People's History of England. London, Lawrence and Wishart, 1945.

Ollman, Bertell. Alienation: Marx's Conception of Man in Capitalist Society. Cambridge University Press, 1976, 2nd ed.

Parker, R. H. and Harcourt G.C. Readings in the Concept and Measurement of Income. Cambridge University Press, Cambridge, 1969.

Pollard, S. The Genesis of Management. Edward Arnold, London 1965.

Raw, Charles. A Financial Phenomenon: An Investigation of the

Rise and Fall of the Slater Walker Empire. Harper and Row, London, 1977.

Robinson, Joan. Further Contributions to Modern Economics. Basil Blackwell, London, 1980.

Sraffa, P. The Production of Commodities by Means of Commodities. Cambridge University Press, Cambridge, 1960.

Steedman, I. and Sweezy, P. The Value Controversy. Verso Editions and New Left Books, London, 1981.

Tinker, A. M. "Towards a Political Economy of Accounting." Accounting, Organizations, and Society. Vol. 5, No. 1, pp. 147-60, 1980.

Tinker, A.M. "Theories of the State and the State of Accounting: Economic Reductionism and Political Voluntarism in Accounting Deregulatory Theory," Journal of Accounting and Public Policy. Vol. 3, No. 2, 1984.

ABOUT THE CONTRIBUTORS

ABRAHAM J. BRILOFF

Abraham Briloff was born and educated in New York City where he completed his baccalaureate and master's degrees from the City College (now the City University of New York). He obtained his doctorate from New York University.

For approximately twenty years, he has pursued the profession of accountancy as a certified public accountant and as a professor of accountancy at Baruch College. In 1976 he was named Emanuel Saxe Distinguished Professor of Accountancy.

His writing is prodigious. His principal publications include four books: Effectiveness of Accounting Communication (Praeger Press, 1967), and Unaccountable Accounting (1972), More Debits than Credits: The Burnt Investors' Guide to Financial Statements (1976), The Truth About Corporate Accounting (1981), all by Harper & Row. His articles, in excess of one hundred, have appeared in journals for the financial community, the accounting, legal, and educational professions, and for general readership.

Over the years, Abraham Briloff has been invited to lecture to professional and academic audiences on themes of accounting concepts and accountants' responsibilities. He has testified in those areas on behalf of corporate entities and congressional bodies. Such activity reflects his continual efforts to address the central theme of his research - the need for enhancing ethical behavior in accounting practice.

CHARLES E. LINDBLOM

Charles Lindlom was born in California and obtained a B.A. in Economics and Political Science from Stanford University and a Ph.D. from the University of Chicago. He joined the Economics Faculty of the University of Minnesota in 1938 and in 1946 he joined Yale University, where he has remained to this date.

Whilst at Yale, Charles Lindblom has held a number of distinguished positions, including: Yale University, Director, Institution for Social and Political Studies (1974-1981); Guggenheim Fellow (1960-1961), Economic Advisor to the American Ambassador and to the Director of the United States Aid Mission to India (1963-1965); Yale University, Director of Social Science (1968-1970); Yale University, Chairman, Department of Political Science (1972-1974); President, Association for Comparative Economic Studies (1975-1976); President, American Political Science Association (1981).

Charles Lindblom has published numerous books and articles, including the following: Unions and Capitalism (Yale University Press, 1949); Politics and Economic Welfare (with R.A. Dahl, Harper and Brothers, 1953); A Strategy of Decision (with D. Braybrooke, The Free Press, 1965); Politics and Markets: The World's Political-Economic Systems (Basic Books, 1977); Usable Knowledge: Social Science and Social Problem Solving (with D. Cohen, Yale University Press, 1979), and The Policy Making Process (revised edition, Prentice-Hall, 1980).

STANLEY SPORKIN

Mr. Sporkin, General Counsel of the Central Intelligence Agency since May 1981, has had a long career in public service. After graduating from law school, he clerked three years for Judge Caleb M. Wright, Chief Judge of the District Court for the District of Delaware, from 1957 to 1960. Mr. Sporkin then entered the private practice of law in Washington, D.C., with the law firm of Haley Wallenberg and Bader. In 1961 Mr. Sporkin joined the United States Securities and Exchange Commission, initially to work on the SEC's special study of securities markets. In 1963 at the conclusion of his special assignment, Mr. Sporkin became a staff member of the SEC. Between 1963 and 1974 Mr. Sporkin held positions with increasing responsibilities culminating in his appointment as Director of the Division of Enforcement in 1974. Mr. Sporkin held that position until May 1981 when he joined the CIA.

Mr. Sporkin was born in Philadelphia on 7 February 1932.

He received his B.A. degree in 1953 from Pennsylvania State University, where he was elected to Phi Beta Kappa. He graduated from Yale Law School in 1957. Mr. Sporkin was admitted to the Pennsylvania and Delaware Bars in 1958 and the District of Columbia Bar in 1963, and was admitted to practice before the U.S. Supreme Court in 1964. He is also a Certified Public Accountant and serves as an Adjunct Professor of securities law at Howard University School of Law.

In 1979 Mr. Sporkin was a recipient of the President's Award for Distinguished Federal Civilian Service, the highest honor that can be granted to a member of the federal career service. He received in 1978 the Rockefeller Award for Public Service from the Woodrow Wilson School of Public and International Affairs at Princeton University and in 1976 the National Civil League's Special Achievement Award. He has also been presented the Securities and Exchange Commission's Distinguished Service Award and Supervisory Excellence Award. In 1979 Mr. Sporkin was given the Alumnus of the Year Award by Pennsylvania State University. In 1981 Mr. Sporkin received the rank of the Meritorious Executive in the Senior Executive Service for sustained superior accomplishment in management of programs of the United States Government and for noteworthy achievement of quality and efficiency in the public service. In 1984 Mr. Sporkin received the Meritorious Officer in the Senior Intelligence Service Award for sustained superior accomplishments.

TONY TINKER

Tony Tinker was born and educated in London, England. He has held accounting positions with several organizations, including The National Health Service, Shell-Mex and B.P., Unilever Ltd., and The London Playboy Club. He studied for the examinations of the Association of Certified and Corporate Accountants at South West London College and was admitted to associate membership of the Association in 1970 after attaining a national placing in the finals examination. He became a fellow of the Association in 1975.

Tony Tinker obtained a master's degree from Bradford University in 1970 and a Ph.D. from the University of Manchester in 1975. He spent five years as a lecturer in Economic Studies at the University of Sheffield and then joined the University of Washington in Seattle (1977-1978), UCLA (1978-1980), and New York University (1980-1984). Currently, he is a member of faculty of Baruch College, City University of New York.

Tony Tinker is presently chairman of the Public Interest Section and council member of the American Accounting Association. He is on the editorial board and serves as referee for a range of business and social science journals and has published in leading journals of several disciplines.